NO NEWS

90 Poets Reflect on a Unique BBC Newscast

edited by
Paul Munden
Alvin Pang
Shane Strange

No News
Recent Work Press
Canberra, Australia

Copyright © the authors, 2020

ISBN: 9780648685388 (paperback)

A catalogue record for this book is available from the National Library of Australia

All rights reserved. This book is copyright. Except for private study, research, criticism or reviews as permitted under the Copyright Act, no part of this book may be reproduced, stored in a retrieval system, or transmitted in any form by any means without prior written permission. Enquiries should be addressed to the publisher.

Cover image is of the UK-made Lissen LN8109 valve-tube radio from the early 1930s by Electro Mechanic812291 reproduced under Creative Commons 3.0 licence
Cover design: Recent Work Press
Set by Recent Work Press

recentworkpress.com

PROGRAMME

Introduction   11
Paul Munden, Alvin Pang & Shane Strange

PRELUDE

April the 18th   17
Paul Munden

I. SLOW RADIO

Slow Radio   21
Susan Wicks

Take Nothing for Granted…   23
Oliver Comins

Black Easter   24
Alyson Miller

Good Friday, 1930   25
Nathanael O'Reilly

Piano Prayer (April 18, 1930)   27
Jessica Wilkinson

It Has Been Business as Usual   28
Hamid Roslan

Night Music   30
David Clarke

Privilege   31
Caren Florance

Liebestod   32
Stuart Barnes

Undocumented   33
Linda Ashok

What Didn't Happen Today   34
Owen Bullock

What News There Is	35
Tjawangwa Dema	
Letter from Rio de Janeiro to Bethlehem, April 1930	37
Nathalie Handel	
Slow-News Days	38
Anne-Marie Fyfe	
Clearing a Path	39
Moya Pacey	
War Artist	40
Ian Duhig	
The Smoothness	41
Ian McMillan	
Pure Fool	42
Yeow Kai Chai	
April 17, 1930—Nothing to Remember	45
Kimberley Williams	
Olds	46
Cole Swensen	
Waku the Crow and Bilyara the Eagle Discuss the Sighting of the First White People's Arrival Upon Barkindji Country	47
Paul Collis	
Out of Eden	48
Cliff Forshaw	

II. TIME AND TIDE

Time and Tide	53
Tammy Lai-Ming Ho	
What News Abroad i'the World	54
Maura Dooley	
Blades	55
Marc Nair	

Haibun for Sister Julian   56
Katrina Naomi
Petard   57
Tishani Doshi
Flatmates   58
Matthew Stewart
Office Politics   59
Hsien Min Toh
Slow Millennia   60
Aidan Coleman
'The Passage of Time'   61
Jen Webb
Static   62
Paul Hetherington
Slack   63
Philip Gross
Sentence   64
Theophilus Kwek
Push the Button, Hear the Sound   65
Helen Mort
Digging a Hole to the Other Side of the World   67
Ramona Herdman
The Philosopher   68
John Yau
24-hour (No) News (Haiku) Cycle   69
Andy Jackson
Morning Alert   71
Nessa O'Mahony
My Father's Father's News   72
Stephen Knight
Breaking News on the Fifteenth of August 2014   73
Susmita Bhattacharya

Recovery	74
Lisa Brockwell	
Fate	75
Gemma Nethercote Way	
The Uses of Poetry	77
D.W. Fenza	
if I write a poem	80
Jazz Money	
Forty-two Poems I Want to Write	83
Desmond Kon	
Blank Page Meets a Deadline	85
Glyn Maxwell	
Change in the Political Climate	86
Graham Mort	
Tsunami, New Guinea 1998	88
Jennifer Harrison	
Flood	89
Robin Thomas	
Last Will and Testament	90
Ilya Kaminsky	
When I Am Nothing	95
Katherine Lockton	

III. THE NEWS FROM HERE

The News from Here	99
Katharine Coles	
Post-truth	101
Gopika Jadeja	
Unconscionable Conduct	103
Jerzy Beaumont	
Poor Circulation	104
KA Nelson	

News Fast 105
Cassandra Atherton
Sparks Between Wagner and Erasure 106
Martin Figura
Sh:Out 108
Bernice Chauly
Warhol Heritage Day: Composition for Scissors and Piano 111
Oz Hardwick
Easter on the Island 112
Helen Ivory
Cold Tips and Gold Patience 114
Michael Leach
Nothing to See Here 116
Angela Gardner
Love in the Time of New Media 117
Vahni Capildeo
There Is No News 118
Christopher Merrill
Elemental News 119
Tricia Dearborn
A Newspaper Lands in the Ocean 120
Miles Salter
Kairos 121
Priya Sarukkai Chabria
On the border 126
Rachel Blau DuPlessis
Last Small Things 129
Jill Jones
Women's Histories 130
Es Foong
Now Is Not the Time 131
Penelope Layland

2020, year of no denying	132
Robyn Bolam	
Repeat	133
Jordan Williams	
Studies Say Melanin Protect Us from Skin Cancer but Can Also Cause It	134
Pooja Nansi	
Some Flowers Open Only Once for a Night	135
Alice Willitts	
Outer Power	137
Nicholas Wong	
Wheat Field with Crows	139
Andy Brown	
Thumbs up for a No News Day Said the Wattlebird	140
Anne Elvey	
Broken When the Underbrush Moved	142
Alfred A Yuson	
Monsoon-ready	143
Marjorie Evasco	
The Goldberg Variations	145
Anne Caldwell	
The Children	146
Maggie Butt	
No-News World	147
Mookie Katigbak-Lacuesta	
Obsequies	148
Robert Pinsky	
Endling	149
Ranjit Hoskote	
Journey	150
Lydia Kwa	

This Page Intentionally Left Blank 152
Paul Munden, Alvin Pang & Shane Strange
Space-Walker Considers a Broadcast 153
Adrian Caesar

CODA

Headlines 156
Joshua Ip

Notes 160
Biographies 162

Introduction

On 18 April, 1930, at 8.45pm, the BBC announced: 'There is no news.' Piano music played for the rest of the 15-minute bulletin.

So the story goes. On further investigation, it seems there were mitigating circumstances: the date in question was Good Friday; the BBC had no news journalists of its own at the time, relying on news gathered from the press—which did not publish that day. Nevertheless, there had indeed been earlier news bulletins, so the 8.45pm 'blank' would seem to represent a genuine case of there being nothing new to report. The concept intrigued us, and we felt that it would serve as an irresistible focus for a new anthology of poetry, in the mould of other themed anthologies published by Recent Work Press over the past few years. Since the 'event' was 90 years ago, we invited a corresponding 90 poets to contribute. Our geographical spread as editors (in England, Singapore and Australia) is reflected in the variety of poets here assembled—with many other countries also in the mix.

Rather than group poems according to editorial affiliation, we decided instead to make use of their poetic, gravitational pull towards one of three loci: the event itself (Part I); the stark contrast presented by the news of today (Part III); and personal stories grounded in the intervening years—and the passage of time itself (Part II). Naturally, given poets' tendency to 'tell it slant' (to use Emily Dickinson's phrase), the boundaries between these loci are blurred, but we hope they prove useful in navigating this substantial body of work. Joshua Ip's contribution is a natural 'Coda', formed from all the other poems. Paul Munden offers a 'Prelude', as 18 April was his mother's birthday and formed a personal marker apt in the creation of this book.

The concept of 'no news' provoked contributions that 'speak back' to the conceit. If the BBC represented, in some ways, the reach of British global power, then what news from the places where that power was being (silently) prosecuted? Thankfully, some of the work collected in this volume, in its perspectives on history and/or place, illuminates such lacunae.

And, as perhaps expected, there is mention amongst the poems of 'fake news', a concept that came to prominence during the US Presidential Election of 2016, with Donald Trump subsequently applying the term to any story he didn't like, particularly those bearing uncomfortable truths. The age-old tussle between 'opinion' and 'fact' has become heightened, with the rise of social media contributing to confusion, political manipulation—and mistrust. Within social media channels we all too often operate without debate, and sometimes nothing 'pierces / The glorious iridescent bubble / Of our preoccupations', as Katharine Coles' poem puts it so well (p 99). We post our own news, as frequently as we like, and see others respond within seconds (and when a post gets no response at all it can be quite disconcerting). We are fully accustomed to witnessing updates flickering across our screens in real time. Never has the notion of 'no news' seemed more implausible.

*

When we commissioned the poems, no one could have had any idea of the news that would unfold this year, with the spread of the coronavirus. As we head towards 18 April, the day on which we intended to launch the book in York, countries around the world are in lockdown mode, with individuals isolated at home and attending to the news like never before. We are witnessing an almost unprecedented rate of change to our daily lives, and broadcast news—even with its 21st century sophistication—has barely kept up.

As historian Tim Crook states, 'the [BBC] radio news of 1930 was, 'an unselfconsciously amateur operation' which was 'held in contempt by Fleet Street journalists'. It is possible, however, that those journalists saw the writing on the wall:

> The existing news organisations of the day had bitterly opposed any suggestion that radio be allowed to become a real competitor to the press, and it was prepared to insist on the copyright it held on its own bulletins to prevent their being used as a source by the BBC.

Today the BBC has its own news operation of exceptional scope and depth but as a publically funded network it continues to attract criticism from competitors. Charges of political bias are levelled against it from both sides, but one only has to look at the Murdoch press to see bias in its much uglier, pernicious form. Broadcasting news for ideological, financial purposes is not a pretty sight, and political machinations have put the BBC under increasing threat. It has appeared unlikely that it can survive in its current form, funded by a licence fee, and yet the events of 2020 have highlighted how invaluable a public service broadcaster can be. Some countries have despaired at the lack of identifiable, regular, trusted updates to guide them through the crisis, while the BBC has offered constant support.

There was however an interesting occurrence, on Friday 27 March, when the 6pm news summary on BBC Radio 3 produced silence, and classical music once again held sway. For a moment, it felt as if the 90 years had come full circle.

Paul Munden, Alvin Pang & Shane Strange

Prelude

April the 18th

My mother's birthday,
a date I've reflected upon
all my life—a neat four weeks
after my own.
                What was 'news'
to a girl aged nine,
                lost
in a world of make-believe?
Music on the wireless
(as she would always call it)
was preferable, but her gifts
were a greater delight.

She had no piano as a child,
to my knowledge, but gave one
to me. And I sit here now
for a moment's silence
before my fingers articulate
their rhythmic response.

i.m. B.E.M. (1921–1980)

Paul Munden

I.
Slow Radio

Slow Radio

The first time, what they heard was music,
a piano tinkling somewhere in the distance
as if the player had just been dozing,
bending his ear low to the keyboard,
flexing his practised hands.

The second time, they heard footsteps,
an owl hooting in the trees beyond the garden,
a dog barking for no reason—
or was it a fox?—as if something were waiting,
word of it spreading like mould or pollen.

The third time, there seemed to be giggling,
exhalations into darkness, whispers
muffled by hot fingers, breath in the narrow spaces
between mouth and ear, mouth and cheek,
culminating in a soft scuffle.

The fourth time, it was passing traffic,
tyres swishing across wet tarmac.
Then a crunch. Hooting. Sirens
changing tone and gone, their blue lights turning,
something needing to be cut free, or someone.

The fifth time there was a screeching
of brakes, car doors slammed shut, and words
unheard on radio spat out—was it in anger?—
as if someone had finally had it
up to here and said *Fuck off*, and stopped caring.

The sixth time it was almost morning,
the air filled with the noise of queueing
planes as they came in to land, the sound
of drunken singing—*Roll me over in the clover*
close at hand—or was it praying?

The last time there was only buzzing.
They opened their door to silence,
looked up, and knew their listening hours
were over, as if the world itself
were past speech, its unreported day beginning.

Susan Wicks

Take Nothing for Granted…

The evening's routine is dispersed a little by Easter,
but there is still a brew to be poured and family china
waiting on the table. This year spring is slow, not warm,
so a coal fire is burning in the grate, spitting tiny cinders
onto the hearth. From time to time, puffs of acrid smoke
avoid the chimney. They float into the room and merge
with sweet odours emanating from a favoured blend.

Perhaps the news is there already—reported and written,
on spikes and in-trays, awaiting production in a moment,
although something is missing, a sense of importance.
The mid-wife editor, knowing more than he or she should,
believes the right course of action on this day is inaction.
So they all pack up and go out for a drink, or a meal,
or an early return to an unprepared home or apartment.

Or is the failure complete and systemic? An existential crisis
of everything caught perfectly in this simple announcement.
The voice in the wireless gives way to music, the soft notes
allow some listeners to reflect on termination in the moments
they have left. For others, this simple piano playing quietly
somewhere in London is a distraction from all those things
which are passing so swiftly and urgently into oblivion.

Oliver Comins

Black Easter

Grimsby Town beats Birmingham City, 2-1, and no one notices the wreathes ignite during Lamentations, the flames flick-licking across the crackle-dry walls in the breath it takes to fill the locked room with the fury of heat and incense and prayer. Singers in the narthex watch as the attic collapses, a harrowing of hell from the heavens; listen to the smashing of shingles and pews, a threnody that catches in the dark spaces left behind. The morning-after haze might be Chittagong, or the cigars of troops lit in the name of King and Empire, the click-pop of telegraphs, impropriety, and guns. The baby came early for Margaret, number three for the Smiths but one of 62,151 Roberts destined for Bert, Robbie, Rob, Bobbie, Bob, and Bo, the silent generation of censors and lung cancer and the midlife crisis. A typhoon in Leyte sinks two ships, rattles a chimney stone in Hoxton, causes four gulls to fall from the sky; Happy Jack Stivetts dreams one last time of the perfect pitch. In an airlocked London studio, a ten-word announcement before Wagner's *Parsifal* loops from Queen's Hall to sitting room speakers: the story of an idiot boy, obsessed with mother, who does not know, knows nothing, knows not.

Alyson Miller

Good Friday, 1930

Hundreds of millions of worshippers
attended church services around
the world, commemorating Jesus'
crucifixion and death at Calvary.
Believers fasted, wept, kneeled, sang, prayed.
Schools, universities, offices
and shops closed. There is no news today.

Rebels fighting for independence
from harsh British colonial rule,
inspired by the 1916
Irish Easter rising, burned armouries
in Bengal. The administration
imposed martial law. British troops restored
order. There is no news today.

The *Salt Lake Telegram* reports Mrs.
Sarah Robinson Rushton, mother
of two sons and six daughters, fifty-
seven grandchildren, eighty-six great-
grandchildren, and eight great-great-grand-
children, died aged ninety-three of general
debility. There is no news today.

Dolores Caplinger was born
in Virginia. Dolores Black,
Dolores Hollenbach and Dolores
Boring were born in Pennsylvania.
Dolores Gamel was born in New
York. Dolores Rogers was born
in Ohio. There is no news today.

An eighteenth-century wooden church
caught fire in Costești, Romania,
during Easter mass. The roof collapsed.
The narrow door jammed. One hundred

and eighteen souls perished, all but two
children and teens. Fourteen escaped
alive. There is no news today.

Nathanael O'Reilly

Piano Prayer (April 18, 1930)

In Washington D.C., First Lady Lou is recovering from a fall in the White House.

In Rome, the Queen of Sweden's long-ailing body had coughed its last.

In Schiller Park, Illinois, snack cakes are pumped full to bursting with thick banana cream.

Mayakovsky's body has commenced decomposition in the Novodevichy Cemetery.

Rumours circulate that Empress Zewditu of Ethiopia had died of a broken heart.

Gandhi held grains of salt on the beach at Dandi; he urges peaceful protest,

while Surya Sen decrees that 'humanism is a special virtue of the revolutionary'.

Black Easter in Costesti. All the children of the village are dead.

In London, 'Nation shall speak peace unto Nation': *Good evening.*   Let us play.

Jessica Wilkinson

It Has Been Business as Usual

(after the *Singapore Free Press and Mercantile Advertiser,* 18 April 1930)

that the Government policy in regard
to the Singapore Base is to be immediately reviewed
in view of the Pact;

> that I expected seasonal festivities,
> but there were none; that I walked about
> for over two hours without seeing any

person, or even a close imitation thereof;
that a Sikh makes the best soldier
and the finest policeman in the East;

> that fashions for big women
> (by our woman correspondent);
> that the reason for the ejection

was that she was
for a long time in the lounge
without buying drinks;

> that in fact they had become almost barbarian,
> until raised again by Christian culture,
> which is still striving against savage reactions,

but alas! We are preparing for the spring
of the China that modern China
looks back as to a golden age;

> that this is a plain statement of fact and incontrovertible;
> that in the future there will be a limit of time;
> that it was arrant nonsense to talk of throwing over the
>   capitalist system,

find instant relief;

      in this standard,
      what earthly chance have these boys
      to find employment against

the two hundred odd boys of other nationalities,
especially when offices advertise
for vacancies with the proviso:

      'Chinese and Eurasian preferred'?;
      that outwards,
      homewards,

it had become the law
of life to him by this time,
more or less parallel.

Hamid Roslan

Night Music

Across the copse, breeze in the farthest leaves—
a tremulation in sap, a hum in its wires.
Fungal networks whispered. In dark eaves
an owl conjured itself like smoke from the fires
of its own owl-eyes. Deep in the byre's
lee, ground twitched with scarab songs
that unmade every floral mound of dung.

From the house by the ashen track, no voices called—
its Formica radio quivered to *Clair de lune*,
and in the porchlight's penumbra, soft moths scrawled
their hazard lines across a milky lawn.
On haunches, at field's edge, a hare was tuned
to the hedgerow's electric rumour, and in his lair
a dog fox stirred, night-signals bristling fur.

David Clarke

Privilege

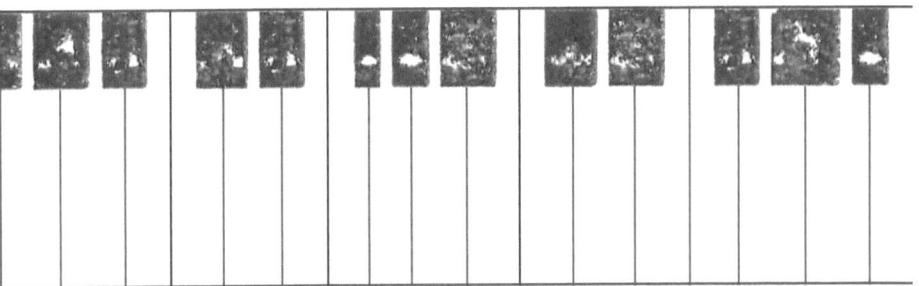

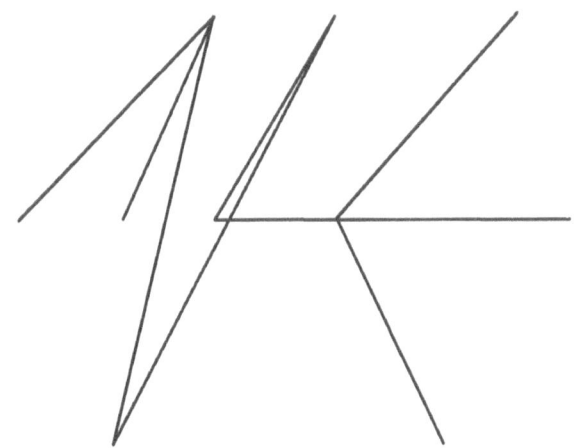

Caren Florance

Liebestod

i.m. Sandy Mitchell

    'There is no news' was the diplomatic
overture to the polychromatic
Wagner drama that later illumined household
and neighbourhood. Our good Fridays were manifold.
Wireless on, faces in books, somatic

praxis. Sudden static: 'Symptomatic.'
Three-month interlude, monochromatic.
An allied GP unloosened my stranglehold:
    'There is no news.'

The Facebook DM was aromatic
as mustard gas; semiautomatic
German pistol: 'Love-death.' I'll forever enfold
him as *Parsifal* enfolds *Tristan und Isolde*
(I hold the Prelude's first chord, chromatic:

```
       t   h   e   r   e
       i           s
       n           o
       n   e   w   s)
```

Stuart Barnes

Undocumented

There is no news
  of

  the volcano that fought her own anger
  the sting that lost to hamartia
  the roads that were born to lead the lost
  the door that finally spoke of consent
  the letter that pawned its shoulder
    to carry someone's grief
  the plum that ached for warmth
  the wasteland that promised good harvest

There is no news
  of

  the man who drilled his chest for songs
  the woman who was prettier than the night
  the children who stitched the village to life

There is no news
  of

  the birds if they've returned
  to their withered feathers

Linda Ashok

What Didn't Happen Today

A chubby-legged poodle called Brandy didn't waddle across the oval

A gull didn't soar slow and alight

A woman didn't stand and gaze, waiting for her dog to return

The sun didn't set over Black Mountain, fiery orange, burning yellow

A mynah didn't glide low across the path, or reach up to take seeds

A man didn't scrape a peppermint eucalypt for menthol, or get confused by a stick in the shape of a water dragon; didn't savour the cool evening air and the single, long, whooping magpie call; didn't grate extra cheese for semi-final night, pick lemon balm from the cracks between tiles in the courtyard, or notice layers of grey in the ashen dark, ticking over like a faceless clock

Day didn't lime the clouds, the clouds drift south-west, burgundy salvias flower again

Owen Bullock

What News There Is

And obviously on that day that accepted mode and convention meant that there was nothing of significance that the public was meant to hear.
—Helen Boaden

And maybe this is the problem with empires: how they have forced us to live in a world lacking in mermaids
—Kei Miller, *The Law Concerning Mermaids*

this is what I know
that when I bring the news
the story runs through me like water
while Mma Aku's fingers nimbly pick dried stalk from desiccated bean leaves
news for whom? she says
fifteen minutes and not a word to fill it?
and piano music? who made that choice
that should've been the news
would've been if we'd heard there was a shortage

Mma Aku's thighs are pressed together before her
like a beached mermaid when she asks
what privilege would let you believe
this news
that not one person woke to fetch water from across a city's length
or to die
what news of them
tell them there was nothing but a song to fill the air that day
that not one person made a thing
or broke it—a basket, a promise, this cup
that everything stayed the same
and that even then
that was the same thing as unremarkable

I want to say this is why
the young make news of every thing
why they re-member themselves so constantly
instead I say
that even the pinch of a misplaced gusset in a public setting

is news
to the one who can do nothing to ease discomfort
that for a time the stubbed toe is the mind's only story
until a sharper song comes along

perhaps we are both right Mma Aku says
her shaking head a slow song of beads
what parses passes for memory here
what news there is
seeks a different ear

the leaves are boiling
but Mma Aku cannot let it rest
in what language is there a lack of stories
the trouble is
all our days we cannot remember how we got here
so we trust men in dinner jackets to tell us
and the day belongs to men like that
and their guessing

I wait for her to say what she always says
that the mouth is a shoe
it moves, it tramples and it turns
I sense she's running her tongue
through the small gap in teeth
what differs is the heart's eye
how it decides whose story is worth telling
say it's been this way since before my grandfather was a cobbler
say that
and let's call the whole thing
a lapse in judgement

Tjawangwa Dema

Letter from Rio de Janeiro to Bethlehem, April 1930

Rio is mourning. We can't see our spirits in the wind, our faces in other faces, nor our prayers on the last shore.

Cardinal Joaquim Arcoverde de Albuquerque Cavalcanti died today. Allah yerhamo. I went to pay meus pêsames, as they say here. He was the first Latin American and Brazilian cardinal. I saw him once, asked if god was enough?

Light a candle for him at the Nativity Church. How many words do we need to convey loss? How many losses must we live to find peace?

I am surrounded by Bethlehem mother-of-pearl and olive wood handicrafts—Jesus on the cross, the Virgin Mary, saints, shepherds.

Tell me what the olive trees are telling me from far away?

Tell me what happened today? You were supposed to have met the municipal members on April 18th. The Handal brothers told me the British are stopping our trading, reducing our exportation?

Tell me, are the British helping settlers invest, and discriminating the indigenous population?

Since the 1929 riots, I have grown more anxious.

I received a letter from Antoine in London telling me the British news doesn't report what is happening in Palestine. Who will tell us if we will hear the hum of those who sleep by the sea? Who will tell us if the hours will be too heavy to carry our deaths?

Who will tell us the news?

Tell me all they haven't said. Of the skies they steal and the sanctuaries they empty, of the great whispers they use to split us apart.

Tell me, so we can remind them their music can't create or drown us.

Nathalie Handel

Slow-News Days

Where I was raised we knew no slow-news
days, no fillers in the half-hour
that gripped my father
with the God's-honest-truth-of-it,
its urgency told out in street-scene,
barricades, an arms cache, baton & canister.

We ached for a Cage-like 4'33"
a mute prelapsarian antechamber,
no siren, blast or ricochet,
no automatic report;
a week, a day, one single bulletin,
without wakes, cortèges, interments;
a tea-time when no names start queueing
to make tomorrow's bullet-points & summary.

We longed for a six-o'clock when our news
would be indistinguishable—
a grandfather asleep at the wheel,
the exam-board getting it wrong third year
in a row, shuttle launches, a dictator toppled.

Longed for that clear day when a Marathon runner
arrives at the Royal Avenue checkpoint
barefoot amid broken glass
with a war zone's truth
on his 26.2-mile expression
& Friday shoppers stoop to catch
his collapsing death-rattle:
I have nothing… I have nothing to report.

Anne-Marie Fyfe

Clearing a Path

Send me oranges
why don't you send me

                  oranges,
                  nuts, or silk stockings?

I am browned off.
No news. No company.
                  (Only Sweepy, the cat)
 & this war is so cruel.
                From your devoted wife,
underlined three times with a tough nib & finished with a
line of eleven black kisses.

She didn't send the photograph he'd asked for.
I only had half a dozen and they all went like lightning.
You will have to wait
                until I get taken again.

Her letter finds you at Castel Gandolfo, 1944,
in an orange grove
           fruit fallen
                brown as burnt khaki.

She asked you for silk stockings & orangesandnutsand
today, I'm watching you
clearing a path for her, yours
the only path that goes so far through snow
from the house at least
one hundred yards to the bus stop.

                                                Moya Pacey

War Artist

She sculpted her son's image from his absence,
and it was this that came home to her every week
where she waited on the hill watching for his train.

She watched steam rhyme its arrival and departure
like breath for a poem the best words might yet fail
let alone these hanging in the air, hid in the cloud.

She composed a new song from her son's silence
that echoes round these hillsides and their home.
You can hear it in the white spaces of this page.

She painted with pure light, like a photographer,
which contains all colours, flagmakers' palettes
and more, that light which is the shadow of God.

Ian Duhig

The Smoothness

Feel this. Come on, lean over, feel
My forehead. Feel. Smooth, isn't it?
A smoothness lurking somewhere
At the placid, still edge of the real.

No lines. No lines at all on my head.
A complete lack of headlines. No,
What would you call it now, detail
In headlines. Smoothness instead

Of the striations news always brings,
The ploughed furrows, rutted roads;
Just this blankness, like the tiny silence
Of the dawn before a first bird sings.

Ian McMillan

Pure Fool

For my infant father, reconstituting the non-events of 18 April 1930

'Are you not of more value than they?' A baby, in all innocence, begins like any other. Thirty-eight years before your fourth child comes to this world, here you are, my dear Father, birthed in the manger of my imagination which neither sows nor reaps nor gathers into barns. A few months old (exact age inconclusive, as no record of your birthdate exists) and naked as we came, you're cradled in the arc of your mother (or that of your aunt, elder sister, grandma, who knows). Likelier you're already sound asleep, alone in a cradle, or swung gently in a hammock, sleep pendulous, chest rising and falling in bed at 3 or 4am, in Qionghai county in an island in south China... while half a globe away, over wireless radio, amniotic piano is played for the rest of a 15-minute segment after the announcement—10 simple words—is made by an announcer dressed in a spiffy dinner jacket on Good Friday; a statement so morally well-intentioned and delivered matter-of-fact, that speaking it now feels like outrage, and afterwards, the channel flits back to live broadcast from the Queen's Hall in Langham Place, London, where *Parsifal*, the last completed opera by German composer Wilhelm Richard Wagner, is being performed for an audience dressed to the nines. Details are scant as to the cast and set of that performance but a scan of the orchestral instrumentation promises an august presence: flutes, oboes, English horns, clarinets, bass clarinets, bassoons, contrabassoons, trombones, tubas, trumpets, tenor drums, church bells, harps and strings, as well as an onstage thunder machine used in the dramatic destruction of a castle. Boooooom! Coincidentally, Wagner has conceived the opera on a Good Friday too, in April 1857, in a cottage in Zurich called the Asyl (German for 'Asylum'), but even then that memory is unreliable, and it might not have been a Good Friday after all, but 'just a pleasant mood in Nature which made me think, "This is how a Good Friday ought to be,"' recalls the composer, whose source inspiration is *Parzival*, a 13th-century epic poem by German knight Wolfram von Eschenbach, and based on the story of the Arthurian knight Parzival (or Percival) and his quest for the Holy Grail. Wagner has chosen the spelling 'Parsifal' for his opera in recognition of the Arabic origin of the word: 'Parsi' and 'Fal' meaning 'pure (or poor) fool'. So begins another journey, a decade later: As a boy you leave behind your own family to set sail on a boat for the Southern Seas, fleeing the Dai-Nippon Teikoku Rikugun (Imperial Japanese Army) marching from the north... but for now, your heart mirrors the ebb and flow of blood-dimmed tides, and the soft piano playing out its discreet notes across the Western Hemisphere, while closer to us, 36-year-old schoolteacher Surya Sen from Chittagong (in modern-day Bangladesh) leads 65 students, under the banner of the Indian Republic Army, in an uprising against the Empire. At 10pm, one group of six, led by Ganesh Ghosh, storms the police armoury, while another group comprising 10 members, led by Lokenath Bal, takes out the auxiliary force armoury in the Bengal Presidency of British Raj, but, as fate would have it, no ammunition is found. The rebels gather outside the burning police armoury where Sen, sharp in a pristine white khadi dhoti and a long coat topped with a stiff Gandhi cap, makes a military salute and hoists a national flag, thereby declaring the founding of a Provisional Revolutionary Government, amidst shouts of 'Inquilab Zindabad' ('Long Live the Revolution' in Hindustani) and 'Bande Mataram' ('I praise thee, Mother' or 'I praise to thee, Mother' in Bengali). The latter cry is lifted from an ode to the motherland penned by novelist-poet-journalist Bankim Chandra Chatterjee in the 1870s; and later adopted as the National Song of India in October 1937, prior to the end of colonial rule in August 1947. With army reinforcements from Calcutta hot on their trail, the revolutionaries take off before dawn and head for the Jalalabad Hills, looking for somewhere to hide, while more than 6,000 km to the west, hundreds of devotees have already congregated at their own haven at 6pm for Good Friday service: a wooden 18th-century church in Costesti, a small town in Arges County, Wallachia, in south Romania. Within 48 square metres, singers and children huddle, some elders in the narthex, and parents listening from the outside, rapt in song and revelry. During Lamentations, a spark is lit when a candle-flick reaches a wreath braid. It's quickly extinguished, but unbeknownst to all, wreaths in the attic have also caught fire... Alas, the church door, with an open width of only 60cm, is bolted, trapping 130 people. Within a few minutes, dozens die from smoke inhalation, or burns, and then the shingle roof gives way... Only 14 people eventually make their way out, two of them succumbing to injuries afterwards, and altogether 118 lives perish on a day seared into Romanian psyche as 'Black Easter'… but for now, someone in the Empire's headquarters states nothing of note and puts on a recording of ivory tinkling which masks an ocean of burping, snoring, farting, crying, as an infant, woken, peers up towards a round, blurry, godly face whose lips shape words one can't quite comprehend yet, on a Good Friday, not unlike today, or tomorrow, oblivious to 'birds of the air' circling home, armouries and churches up in flames, flags ripped and unfurling, the rancid smell of charred wood and flesh, someone else, who sees the butt-ends of his days and ways, running up the hill, free for the first time and the last, a refugee in his own country stolen by another.

Yeow Kai Chai

April 17, 1930—Nothing to Remember

One day before the BBC announced no news and played piano music for the duration of the broadcast, my *dziadzi* turned thirteen. This was not news either. What could this youth, first generation of Polish parents, offer? Born wearing a blue collar and built tall and wide like the Ford pickup he drove throughout my childhood, what could Mitch bring to a pre-war world that it didn't already have?

He'd live sixty more years and tell his grandchildren stories of selling apples from a cart during the Depression. And when a grandchild was home sick, he'd crush by hand the ice that he'd packed into the glass with Vernors ginger ale. He'd cover our eyes and let us steer the riding mower while sitting on his lap cutting across a half acre of Michigan green. By the end of his life, he'd have three teeth to chew on pickled pigs' feet.

He'd sleep most of those six decades in a single bed in a separate room from his wife and die just before the Pope blessed their 50th anniversary. When he needed to communicate, a grandchild carried the message. On his death card, the 23rd psalm.

Was it a lifetime of wanting that made him down the wine he stored in a thermos in the bed of the Ford? Mother Mary and a compass floated on his dashboard as we grandchildren swiveled on the bench seat waiting for him to drain his red cup at the side of the road. *I shall not want.*

Mitch's life was no news. Nonetheless, I am present to report it.

Kimberley Williams

Olds

The oldest tree
             in the world is thought to be
something seen
             (you saw a ghost but couldn't hold it)
P. longaeva
             some accident 5,062 years ago in California
somewhere
             something green turns to stone
and yet goes on,
             the oldest intentionally planted
by Zoroaster
             a cupressus sempervirens, some
5,000 years ago,
             the Sarv-e Abarkuh, as it is known
in the shade
             of which the oldest tree in Europe
lives in a graveyard
             in Wales some 4,000 years later,
the Llangernyw Yew
             first took root
among flint and boats of stone—

but not all trees
             grow alone—there are clonal groups
(look up the term)
             that go back 80,000 years
(think mushroom)
             cf. Pando, South-Central Utah
or a single
             Norway spruce finding itself ironically
9,550 years later
             still in Sweden.
It's a very slight ache
             but we still wake up
startled by light
             forcing an entry.

Cole Swensen

Waku the Crow and Bilyara the Eagle Discuss the Sighting of the First White People's Arrival Upon Barkindji Country

Here:
not the news

  There:

Bilyara: What's that funny smell, Waku.? *Wom-boo?*
Waku: Hmm. Yes, Wom-boo-stink. . .

Waku: What's that there, Bilyara? Wom-boo?
Bilyara: *Ahh. Hmm. Ugly. . .

What's that sound?
Black lightening? Thunder?

Bang, bang. . .

Cold Fire.

Barkindji feet did not have time to stand, nor could Barkindji feet outrun Yarraman, the day the fires burned out. A powder-burn smell, and molten lead lingered a while, Murrdie spirits flew to Biamai. Barkindji fires shot dead—and white ash changed colours, red, when Barkindji Murrdies turned into Wom-boo. . . The Birthing Place cried cold in ice wind, and then gave up her purpose to memories. Barkindji Murrdie Wom-boo spirits lost their homeland in bullets grey, and, through dead smoke.

  A new land spread open for the taking—
  Price: Free to the 'Settler'.

Paul Collis

Out of Eden

        I saw that apple still glowing in the tree,
        the deadline (thank God!) at least was not today.
        But sure as Hell, He'll put it all down to me.
        Once that fruit falls, it's headlines all the way.

The brandished sword of God before them blazed...
Flood, Drought, Famine, Plague, the ceaseless Wars;
calendars, blood-lettered to the End of Days.

*They hand in hand with wandering steps and slow...*but, of course
once out there, they won't be coming back;
from up on high they'll wait each Solstice out,
tick off Millennia that dawn in vain,
peering anxiously at their falling sky
(the columns of their world held up by hacks).

No Rapture. No spaceship to beam them up. No news.
All History's just a stuttering déjà-vu.
He sees their futures, yet swears e leaves them free:
The world was all before them, where to choose...

        He drags that old defence out every time.
        (Match of the Day: you watch but know the score.
        It doesn't mean you rigged the game.) I'm not so sure.

        It will all come: hot metal, telegraph,
        red-tops, rolling news, uncoiling spools, but first

that red bulb glows: studio silence. He eyes the dials,
flicks switches, slides the dimmers, checks tape-hiss, smiles.
He's used to splicing rushes from when the Future starts.
Sits back, already waiting for what's just about to break.

Through Eden took their solitary way...
He's made this up so many times before:
the endless parallel worlds He tipped awry.
From wireless Eden, right through each family tree,
that thirst for knowledge will soon come down
to celebrity gossip, fake news, the racing tips.
That shining apple, always rotten to the core,
falls, and what's really rolling now is all that world,

the one that's just about to crash the pips.

Cliff Forshaw

II.
Time and Tide

Time and Tide

Our faces glow in front of a row
of lit globes. In the shopping mall,

where we stand—
other lovers we have replaced

had also stood, counting cities
they knew

condensed into dots,
transient in their borders.

Waves somewhere keep up
an unfathomable dance,

stars revise schedules, every summer
lengthens, becoming an elegy.

Maps and globes are oblivious
to an ephemeral celestial event

that we will or will not witness.
So much depends on what is fleeting,

what isn't known, and how eager
the world turns on us by forgetting.

Tammy Lai-Ming Ho

What News Abroad i'the World

> *—There is scarce*
> *truth enough alive to make societies secure; but*
> *security enough to make fellowships accurst: much*
> *upon this riddle runs the wisdom of the world. This*
> *news is old enough, yet it is every day's news.*
>
> Measure for Measure, *Act III, Scene II, Vincentio*

Not the gilded rise and fall of shares or bonds
not the coups and famines, fevers, wars,
nor tides' diurnal ebb and flow on slipping shores
a shuck of ringpulls, tampons, seaweed fronds
those crumbling, trembling outlines of our world.
No, nothing to write Home about.

Maura Dooley

Blades

My brother has made a box
for used razor blades.
Scrap plywood, some glue,
a brace of interlocking joints.

The blades slip like coins
into his piggy bank, a one-way
savings plan with no plug
at the bottom for rainy days.

In the bathrooms of older houses,
he says, there would sometimes be
a slot cut in the wall for used blades;
I think about hidden bodies.

Years later, while renovating,
a small hill of blades showers
on an unsuspecting foreman
like old newspaper clippings,

the details rusted, the razor's edge
now a dull scrape, yet something
nicks at memory; an archive of loss
in foam and clean shaven chins.

Who wants to carry blades around
all the time? It's far easier to throw
these things into a hole in the wall
and pretend no one was ever there.

Marc Nair

Haibun for Sister Julian

It was as if one of our roles as young Catholics was to provide the priest at Our Lady Star of the Sea with news. Did he enjoy guessing which minor misdemeanour was done by which girl? Or were we, as I suspected, in plain view through the grille as we spoke, one after another, into the side of his face, his bristly sideburns, into his large ear, perfectly framed. Each week, clutching my white plastic rosary, I knelt, leaning towards that ear, those sideburns, whispering my sins—I'd hit my sister or eaten her sweets—waiting to become a better six-year-old.

One morning, I told Sister Julian I had nothing to confess. I'd tried really hard that week. I'd washed up, helped my sister with reading, I'd even learnt a psalm. The nun said: *You must have done something, child?* I searched each day. No, I could think of nothing. I imagined the silver halo that was shining above my head, balanced perfectly between the regulation dark blue ribbons of my bunches.

The nun shattered this image: *Well, you have to give the priest something.* Some priests, it seems, don't like silence, or want to hear the gulls outside, they just want another whispered, mini headline. I waited, obedient, breathing in the smoulder of incense. Sister Julian raised her pale blue eyes to heaven. *My child, if you've really done nothing wrong, which I doubt, then tell him this.* Her words fired down at me.

'But I can't say that. I didn't do it.' It was no good. *You have to confess something. Tell him what I've told you to say. And may the good lord bless you for your sins.*

Forgive me, Father
for I have sinned. I burnt down
the school's changing rooms.

Katrina Naomi

Petard

After you were banished to the desert for months, you came home
to find the house occupied. A stranger had moved in and befriended
the dog. Three families of squirrels had built nests in the shuttered

windows, and termites were hard at work in the bathroom, building
a cathedral of sand. The stranger was in the planter's chair reading diaries
and love letters you'd left behind. There was a vodka martini in a chalice,

wind chimes working their best John Denver rendition from the porch.
When the stranger saw you, he said, Wife, welcome home, and for a moment—
confusion. You were not one of those poet-saints whose homes and tombs

were as moveable as their desires. You had not offered up these rooms and said,
You have no bed, take mine. You have no family, be mine. Supper was laid out
on a yellow tablecloth and there was even a vase of bougainvillea drooping

into the soup. It had been so long since you'd seen clouds so the stranger and you
walked out to the beach to marvel at those cumulonimbi, which in every language
are harbingers, heaped and towering like volcanoes floating low above the sea.

The stranger opened his arms as though gathering an imaginary bouquet
of flowers, as if to say, Thanks for all this. It means a lot. Your heart exploded
with its own goodness and exploded again when it considered all it might lose

or might already have lost. You thought about that woman in Iceland who joined
the search party to look for a missing woman, who turned out to be herself.
How it is a search everyday. To wince or not to wince. How at academic

conferences on Hamlet you want to talk not about language being rhizomic
or vectorizing the text, but about an aunt who lifts one cheek casually
mid-conversation, to let loose wind, as though it were news rushing to be told.

Tishani Doshi

Flatmates

Saturday night on his own in the block,
no chance to tell her all his latest news,
he chooses the glasses, cups and saucers
for breakfast, piles up juice-veined oranges,
arranges the slivered Serrano ham
and mixes his palette of coffee beans.

Waking to new footsteps down the hallway,
he hooks a toe round the bedpost and waits.
Piss knifes his abdomen. He should join them
at the table, drop her a knowing wink,
but he's only laid two places
and now he's got no news.

Matthew Stewart

Office Politics

I had put in a good word for my friend,
but there were others vying for the seat
and someone brasher trumped him in the end.
It's true, though, that my life won't be as sweet.
We call this new guy Polymer Kelvin; he
survives always, with a gloss like faience.
Just as a storm feels feckless in a lee,
responsibility is held in abeyance.
Although like kimchi this leaves a sour unease,
I fall in line, for power is contagious.
Better modify one's view than ask for mercy.
Compared to an enema, Crohn's disease
is worse—such calculus is not outrageous.
We've got to wear the winning dream team's jersey.

Hsien Min Toh

Slow Millennia

The forgetfulness of sport lingers
in alleyways and bikes-shops. Fewer men
wash smaller cars—
toothless as the chiding of a fridge door.
The sink glitters with fabulous trophies.
Carrier bags of apricots pass
from house to house.
John Lennon appears in the late afternoon
(with Yoko and Julian) pointing
excitedly. There's a new restaurant
opening round the corner with a quiet
Eastern theme. Over the hill
there's a many-roomed mansion: it's white,
on white, on white, on white.

Aidan Coleman

'The Passage of Time'

(SG&KS)

If a dog should bark. If thought should drift like paper fallen from the roof—a brief flutter and then nothing. The moments of the day coil themselves up, a damaged spring, and then tilt slowly to one side.

The event crept up on us, no herald's call to announce its arrival, its leaving. Only its Cheshire smile remained as evidence of its passing. That, and the shadow of its turn, and the ragged ending points I must knit together.

The hens look up from their grain, then retreat to the roost as heavy rain falls, quietly, out of a blue sky. I can't make sense of it, but you, growing magisterial, announce that the absence of news is the passage of time—as when a dog fails to bark, you say, when the postman does not call.

The cat is asleep in the doorway. I curl up beside her, muted, and we sleep together undisturbed through the events we had not foretold.

Jen Webb

Static

The television's silent. There's static on the radio. Newspapers are blank screens staring at living rooms. There's no gossip in the street. Where people nursed espressos, leaned across counters or idled at fence posts, there's a small, shuffling wind and the faint curling of memory. There's the red swing on which a girl climbed into the sky. That was yesterday. The new apartment block rises, and the jutting calligraphy of a clothesline is writing something indecipherable on blue. There are clouds the apartment window sees. The lorries that rolled in, the wire that stretched, the stations established at the main intersections are ghostings. So much heat and dust. As the wind pushed clouds across the bay's famous vista; as boys and girls straddled their bicycles and were daredevils dropping down the long hill, so something arrived like an elongated shout. Land and air took it up. Men and women gathered disbelief in their houses and cars. Questions sat on their lips like worms.

Paul Hetherington

Slack

The shock
        of the not. One moment, the slew
of the hundred-mile-heavy Severn leans into the arms of its bend,
so slow
        I've taken it for stillness, then
a jolt. As if a clock I'd never noticed ticking, or the river flowing,

stopped.
        Betweentime: between gravities,
the tide's, so intimately grappled with the river's
it could pass for peace...
                And then the surface blisters,
upwells, hauling gulls and driftwood back upstream.

But it's the pause...
        As if one, any, day,
all this could stutter to a halt: the last few drips of incident
before
        their gradual, great un-happening
as they slip from our grasp. How Things Are

folds back into itself, around us. A dream, we say...
and to think that we called it a future.
                But not yet.
Another rolling headline starts out, on its way
to 'Nothing'. Judders. Gets no further
                than 'Not...'

Philip Gross

Sentence

There's a scientific explanation
for most things
                like how life, as they say,
flickers into view moments from the end
or how the soul slips the body briefly—
a sneeze, then dark—but
                for what he saw
that early bright afternoon as it fell
with a clang about him, sky cold as steel
flinching from the sea as if in shock
and the waves
              with a dash of alchemy
turning to iron as he was, then wasn't
a shadow stretched over their salt surface
has still not been found
                any known cause
nor sequence from which we might begin
to derive some hypothesis, some guess
towards a truth…
              no, merely the report
of his mouth which was seen, as he toppled
from the bow into a stretch of channel
uneasily held
            between two territories,
to be holding in its yell the start
of some unspoken sentence, an opening
that could be imagined
              by some of those
who saw the shape of him falling, and knew
something of the deep that would come,
to be the same syllable
              that they too
heard, too often, and hated, and understood.

Theophilus Kwek

Push the Button, Hear the Sound

Listen to the lorikeet's whistling song.
Can you hear the call of the mynah bird?
Can you hear the flamingoes in the water?
Can you hear your small heart next to mine
and the house breathing as it holds us?
Can you hear the chainsaw start, the bones
of our neighbour's eucalyptus breaking?
It's summer, high, emptied. Listen to the ground,
giddy with thirst. Listen to the dog shit
on the lawns, the murderous water boatmen
skimming the green pond. Can you hear
the roses rioting on the trellis? Can you
make a noise like a cheeky monkey? There are
sounds your book lacks names for. Can you
hear the sleepless girls in Attercliffe?
Can you hear the aspirin of the sun dissolving?
Listen to the casual racists in the family pub.
Listen to the house Shiraz I drink as if
it's something's blood. Listen to my fear,
blooming in the vase of my chest
and listen to how I water it. Can you hear
your grandfather's lost childhood? Can you hear
the suburban library shutting? The door closing?
The books still breathing? O can you hear
the budget tightening? It's almost dark.
Listen to the noisy penguins on the ice.
Listen to my late night online purchases.
Orange lipstick. High waisted bikini briefs.
Types of plant that will never die. Listen
to your half-sister hissing to her friends at 2am.
You hang up. No you hang up. Listen
to the panic in their emojis. Can you hear
your father lighting his first cigarette?
Can you hear the foxes mating all the way
to oblivion? Their sounds are inhuman,
too human, scaling the high fences,

pressing our windowpanes. Listen
to the utter indifference of the stars.
The night is full of holes and we
grate our bodies against them.
Can you hear that, Alfie? Can you hear me
holding you, closer than my life?
Listen to The Trout by Schubert.
Listen to the blackbird's chirpy song.
Listen to this waltz by Paganini.
Listen to the stage as we walk clean
off the front of it, into the audience,
the pit, the mute orchestra.

Helen Mort

Digging a Hole to the Other Side of the World

Every house I remember, my father made a pond.
Long evenings digging, back late from work.
They spangled with whirligig beetles
and pondskaters skittering. Waterlillies flowered.
A lone duck repeatedly visited one.
There was the seasonal dredging of algae,
the learnt kindness of leaving the dreck on the edge

for imperceptible creatures to creep back down
into their lives—then chucking the dried crusted gunk
onto the compost. At garden centres
we inspected liners, water-plants, pumps.
He never said anything about desperation.
In winter he'd go out with a fag and a hot pan
to rest on the ice and melt a circle for breathing.

Ramona Herdman

The Philosopher

He sacrificed the vulgar prizes of life but his eyes danced with velvet spleen
He threw out phrases of ill-tempered humor but trod the path of primrose dalliance
He was often empty of thought but remained entangled in paradox
He gave away his youth by the handful but hurrying thoughts clamored for utterance
He was profoundly skeptical but utterly detached from any sign of obstinacy
He went hot and cold but would fall into the blackest melancholies
He writhed with impotent humiliation but his blank gaze chilled you
He smiled with fatuous superiority but was often stunned and uncomprehending
He made a loathsome object but was afflicted with high levels of mental depletion
He delivered a series of monosyllabic replies but parts of him throbbed dangerously

John Yau

24-hour (No) News (Haiku) Cycle

before dawn   your shadow begins
its slow climb out of you

quick-witted   the silvereye
drinks from a leaf   leaves when you move

morning   without thinking   you breathe
the world

it hurts   a memory of driving from the hospital
like a broken rib

tactless   this mug   lamp   mirror
keep crying for her to return

a single cloud   softens the room   obscures
the clock

        the heft of her body   impresses the ground

        tired of seeing things   you put away the book

gusts of hot   dry wind
trees flail   panic

        …   …

now you don't know what isn't news
the temperature at the Svalbard Seed Vault   rising

return from a walk   exhausted
from carrying yourself

your bones
a wind chime

one hundred miles inland   earth swells and currents
your small craft   adrift

the windows are grimed   screens flicker   but elsewhere
is closing in

at the kitchen sink   you lift from the water
a clear mind

drought   thoughts of the future
the back door won't stay shut

hot   still   nightfall   suddenly noticing
the absence of insects

        you with the face   water running in your veins

another siren   fades into the horizon
tinnitus returns

midnight   only so long you can stand
before your shadow   climbs back into you

Andy Jackson

Morning Alert

for my brother, Donal O'Mahony

Through December's dark days
when the solstice stopped
and breaths were held,
I'd picture you striding
through empty corridors.

Then the first ping,
a phone vibration on a desk,
the morning text landing
with indicators you inscribed
with intensive care.

We'd weigh your phrases:
parse '*stable*' against
'*critical*' or '*holding his own*',
the woods he wasn't out of,
what the consultant knew.

We hoarded each report:
traded them like commodities
till we could verify ourselves
the monitor-blinking data,
the pulsing LED heart.

Hours bled into days
drained into weeks;
a world turned,
your morning alerts
our only currency.

Nessa O'Mahony

My Father's Father's News

I bolted the door; the news slipped through the letterbox.
The curtains were drawn but outside the news was calling,
Calling me down to the street in the dark
In a voice that was rising and falling.

The news on the street was hiding its face.
What manner of news would act like that?
Hiding its face in a shadowy corner
With a turned-up collar and a broad-brimmed hat?

I took to my bed and I put out the light
But the news in the hallway was singing and singing
Too loud to accept and too long to ignore,
The news and its terrible, terrible ringing

Sang in the hallway, sang in the otherwise quiet street
A melody both cruel and clear
—Too clear, too insistent, too dark to forget,
And I haven't yet.

Stephen Knight

Breaking News on the Fifteenth of August 2014

*'Come in. Have a seat. I'm afraid
it's not good news.'*

I'm not surprised. When the ultrasound
throws up shadows and the nurse
touches my arm—does not smile or make
eye contact—it's not usually
good news.

I process this reality. A slow burn down
the back of my throat. My brain shouting,
'Your body has let you down.' I listen to the drone
of voices: Speculations. Assurances.
Treatment Plans.

Suddenly I recall from the news feed
this morning: A bottle discovered in a
shipwreck. Two-hundred-year-old spirit
Perfectly preserved in the depths of the Baltic. Safe
to consume.

I hold on to that image. Oh! to drink from that
relic—just one sip. If only for a moment
to be freed from this crushing weight. Away from
the cold reality to an illusion of
welcome relief.

Susmita Bhattacharya

Recovery

Years spent looking, will it ever be found?
I don't think I will get that phone call,

be brought in to look at speckled footage,
faint blooming phantom of cloud and grain

like those polite ultrasounds that bring nothing
but pain; no heartbeat detected.

I have sponsored the search, given it my all,
sunk buckets of money in dubious technology,

submarine and sonar, robot at the cutting edge.
Nothing has come to the surface.

No bodies to bury, no tin-can fuselage,
no black box comfort.

Wedged in a place light cannot reach,
though nothing is wasted there.

Now it feeds a colony of creatures
without eyes but plenty of teeth.

Lisa Brockwell

Fate

The flowers
in the dining room
are always dying.

Most mornings
you think of nothing
but how much longer

your life is than theirs.
Some afternoons
you remember

the still, vined heat
of the garden,
the birds singing—

his hands you knew
like earth
and heft of clay,

his hand
sudden and gripping
your pale arm

as you reached
for the cage.
In this place

there is a woman
who sings ancient
songs to no one.

Night after night
she wanders the halls,
her hair roped

and long as Clotho's.
When will it end?
These songs,

this scent
of waiting ground.

Gemma Nethercote Way

The Uses of Poetry

The cheer of writing that cures no physical hurt.
—Robert Lowell, a note in his journal for February 19, 1973

1.
Mount Carmel was a small
Pennsylvania mining town.
A plane crashed near
the Midvalley Breaker,
& 43 people died.
Through brambles & woods,
all the boys hiked there
to see the wreckage.
But that was years ago.
The mines & breakers
still crushed, maimed,
or killed a few men
from time to time, but
that was just the usual
workaday life. The more
days & trains the valley filled
with heaps of coal, the more
remote the town seemed—far
from history's upheavals.
The news was elsewhere.

1958—Sputnik orbited
the earth; Britain, France,
& Israel fought Egypt
for the Suez Canal—far
from Mount Carmel where
miners dug & criss-crossed
nether plateaus of coal, where
Frank & Stella tended their bar,
where their daughter Esther fell asleep
in a meadow with her back

to a stout tree, where a boy played
with a toy horse beside her.
My mother scolded Esther for
nodding off when Aunt Esther
should have looked after me.
Sleeping is not watching,
my mother said. Hardly
newsworthy, Esther's nap
was one of my earliest
childhood memories.

In 1958, Frank & Stella
turned their backs on God
& then on Mount Carmel.
Their sleepy twelve-year-old daughter
died of leukemia that year.

2.
The sorrow far apart from
history & the news. The anger
of writing that prevents no
official lie. The sighs between words
that move no cloud to douse
houses & trees of embers & flames. The hurt
of writing that puts no leash on a nation's
pet hatreds. The sleeplessness of writing
with impossible revisions. The inverses
& coincidences of writing that show
faces lit by TVs—*too often watching is
a kind of sleeping.* The Venus of writing with
her missing arms. The prayers of writing
that summon no reply.

3.
Frank & Stella stopped going to church.
They sold their tavern, left Mount Carmel,
& moved to a small farm in Aston.
Stella, my grandmother, poured herself

three fingers of whiskey—
'my medicine' she called it—
& drank as she stood by the kitchen window.
She could see her grandchildren playing
on the lawn between the house & barn.

Frank shoveled, hoed, & raked a circle
of soft earth in that lawn. He planted
cannas within a border of Esther's favorite—
zinnias. In summer, orange & magenta
zinnias surrounded the red blossoms
of the cannas. The flowerbed
attracted monarch butterflies, tiger
swallowtails, green humming birds,
& children running round
& round in games of tag.

4.
Upheavals unspoken by reporters.
Workaday people, displaced by leaders
& ignored by history. The long spells of novels
with nuances, threads, semblances, & echoes
that cannot be blown into the confetti &
staccato of social media. The gratuitous
tropes of poetry that restore what history
& the news lack. The small sooty foyer
of a miner's home. A stanza that places
a dying girl beside a tree. The shock
of writing that divides you from
who you were. The puzzles of writing
that connect you to those who use
the same words: *loss, grief, love.*

5.
The shovel that tills the earth.
A circle of zinnias & cannas.

D.W. Fenza

if I write a poem

if I write a poem
it's for the pen
banned from my grandmother's hands

and if I write
it's for our language
stolen from the mouths
of babies in cribs

and if I write a poem
it's so that our children
will read some truth
of their family

and if I write
it's because our story
hasn't been written
        by us
        for us

and if I write
it's because I hate the structure
the capitalism
the greed
the fury

I write a poem
because I love this country

I write a word
because I love my daughter
        who isn't yet born

I write because there is no truth yet
no justice

I write because there is no justice here

and if I write a poem
it's because my mother can't understand

why I weep into the soil
but she cries with me all the same

and if I write
it's because I love a woman
and others do
and cannot write about their love
for their wife

and if I write a word
it's to stop me from burning
within
it's to stop me from burning
the city down
and bearing my breasts
wailing with my clapsticks
a song that boils in my chest
in my soul
that no one has taught me the words to
yet

I write a poem
because I was raised off Country
and I yearn and yearn for a place I don't hold
that holds me

and if I don't write a poem
it's for the magnificence of lightning
of cicadas in chorus
       rhythms too beautiful to capture

and if I don't write a word
it's because I love this country
and all the ways I love her burns

        all the ways I love her burns

and if I don't write
it's because I love a woman
and that is a sacred thing

if I don't write a word
it's because my mother loves me
every way she can

and if I don't write
it's because I can't bring my baby
into a world on fire

and if I don't write
don't think I had nothing to say

        and if I don't write
        don't think I had nothing to say

and if I don't write
it's because this language
these letters
are not worthy

and if I write a word
on the inside of my mouth
in the dust
in the sand
it's because I know
no other truth at all

Jazz Money

Forty-two Poems I Want to Write

1. What Chinese Privilege Looks Like
2. What Foreignness Teaches You About Privilege
3. The Day I Learnt I Had Chinese Privilege
4. The Day I Was Told I Was Too American
5. I Couldn't Teach English Because I Wasn't White
6. They Didn't Even Apologize When They Told Me I Wasn't White
7. The Day Everyone Stopped Joking About Race
8. The Day Everyone Stopped Saying They Weren't Racist
9. The Day I Was Kicked Off A Train In Boston
10. When Wearing Black Stopped Being Derridean Chic
11. It's Both Peony Red And Paloma Picasso Red
12. That Ines De La Fressange Pinkie Ring
13. That Hour Glass Clasp Snaps Into Place, Like My Heart Locket
14. I Remember Ines De La Fressange First Wearing Chanel
15. I Remember Chanel's Over-Priced Magnolia Brooch
16. You Wore That Magnolia Brooch As A Hat Ornament
17. No One Wears Hats In Singapore—It's Too Much Tropics Chichi
18. Singapore Doesn't Have The Allure Of The Maldives
19. Ines De La Fressange The Designer, No Longer The Muse
20. I Remember The Skepticism, Even Derision
21. Ines De La Fressange, Her Own Muse Forever
22. The Art World Can Be The Cruelest Place On Earth
23. The First Third Of My Life, That Baptism Of Fire
24. I Remember When Religion And Art Weren't Two Separate Things
25. Religion And Art Are Not Age-Old Antagonisms
26. This Is A Poem About Our Litany Of Anachronisms
27. Différance Never Took Off The Way Freud's Ego And Id Did
28. Nowadays Everyone Has Anxiety, Or Something
29. It's Okay To Have A Bad Day, And Write A Song About It
30. You Feel Unsettled, I Feel Unsettled, Let's Make Out
31. I Want To Fuck You When You're Manic, Call Me?
32. Fight Or Flight: Suitable Responses To Worrying Triggers
33. Otherness, The Phenomenon You Only Learn About In College
34. Eight Years Living In One Estate, And Knowing People By Name
35. If You're Nice To A Hawker, They Give You Extra Portions
36. Being A Heartlander For The First Time, You Never Thought…

37. Ilo Ilo, The Movie That Dared The Truth
38. Wet Season, The Movie That Furthered The Dare
39. What Migrants Know About Being Othered, And Then Some
40. 'You Don't Realize How Important Representation Is…'
41. 'Until You Realize You've Been Missing It Your Entire Life'
42. That's Awkwafina, And That's One Memorable Quote

Desmond Kon

Blank Page Meets a Deadline

What are you looking at?
I didn't make your deadline.
I don't know what a deadline is,
    you'll have to tell me.

Is it the sort of grin
you've had since you appeared here?
which now of course you hide away,
    you didn't mean it.

Is it that other thing
you look at? when you rear up
away from me and back again
    and cross some stuff out?

I don't know what it is.
I think it brought you here, though.
I'm going to ask it if that's true
    when you're not looking.

I have. I still don't know.
I don't know what its brief shrug
is saying to me, all I know
    is you don't need to.

Glyn Maxwell

Change in the Political Climate

First snow was sent/ barring the hills
        into black and white
as if everything is an argument between
        right and wrong.

Land and sky were welded for days/ a
        cold inordinate seam.
Snow covered the gardens and a wren
        pecked for something

chest-deep in the stuff. One morning sleet
        thin as the shite of a
sick man/ then a slow melt that slid
        away from everything.

And just when we were about to lose
        our minds or find them
that revelatory wand of sun that we
        take for God's love

when seen through westerly cloud or
        immense windows of a
cathedral stained with Christ's eternal offering.
        Then it was New Year

peanuts and pretzels/ glasses of half-dead
        cava/ hugging in a faery
ring/ catching midnight massacres on
        the news/ Big Ben

tolling. We sent not/ knowing whom.
        Everything we'd ever
believed in would infest us now. A new
        era. Lies were not

an issue and they were good for them.
        We mislaid our creed:
crushed grape/ barley malt/ Lethe's sleep/
        prayer's belief in

disbelief. We guessed it was our children
        calling on the phone let
ring until they broke down doors to find
        us gone/ curtains billowing.

Graham Mort

Tsunami, New Guinea 1998

two Japanese kanji: *tsu* 'harbour' and
nami 'wave' seem small enough words for ruin

each storm a gate/mouth   a ransacked greeting
from Dis   or somewhere more unexpected

together   they know the dispassionate stars
that resume their defiant shimmer   tides

that obey yet the moon's circadian
rhythms   saw-fingered waves   coming going

washing away   the muddied bloated thatch
cradling the dull-eyed fishes   belly-up

along the shore   painful palms   still upright
and the reef   jagged with shattered canoes

the moon cannot be responsible for
scavenging dogs in Sissano village—

far from Arop's news   we have much to lose
between starless dawn and the moon's new rise—

a child was swept away by the Bismarck sea
yes   Hilda Degaway survived   was found

alive in the West Sepik mangroves   no
miracle   nothing new from sandy gods

no hand painting birth on a chapel roof—
two small old words   each clear-eyed as a moon

or a sun   together they make nightwater
the sea's distemper   vast stain of the tongue

Jennifer Harrison

Flood

after Ted Hughes

I drown in the thrumming flood,
in the ice-cold heat of ever rising waters.
Waterfowl eye me, creatures
on floating branches, on mountain tops,

peer at me, me out of place. I hurtle
to the edge of the streaming falls, fall
to join the bones of my brothers, sisters
and children. I go down

in the knowledge of my lastness.

Robin Thomas

Last Will and Testament

Because cemeteries are too pricy
I would like to be deposited on a public bench
and not in the earth
but in the middle of September
at the end of wonder:
wrap me in newspapers, darlings,
and run!

I want to live my death
on a public bench
next to a barbershop,
die, when it is time to cut my hair so I can save four dollars!
I was always happy in barbershops.
Now happiness
come blow your nose in my hands—

I want to die on a public bench
those who watch me in
the street
say
something in him wants to be entered and picked clean.

Be careless, life!
Wrap me in newspaper on a park bench
so some enterprising schoolchild
can filch from my eyes
two dimes
and replace them with two US postal stamps.

2.

I, a deaf man, thank
hearing aids
for not working.
How many insults I did not hear!

How my feet hammer the tight drumskin of this quiet!

Planet, kind
illegible
is alone with my body tonight.

*

I know a death that can be explained is not worth dying for—

        on a park-bench, I stoop
the joy of putting one's cheek
to the park bench!
of whispering:
you in whom I do not believe, hello.

(I am talking to you, God since I am afraid to find myself alone)—

I would like
to die while
watching
the sweet floppiness of bodies squeezing themselves into a public bus!

3.

From a park-bench I watch my pregnant wife chase pigeons on the piazza

Katie!
You have got nerve!

In my final 17 hours:
I have so much love, too much love, I cannot control myself!

Plan A:
I shoot myself. And the earth is mine.

but the earth has never been mine!
Those who say the planet is theirs should pay higher taxes!

*

Katie and I are kissing at 3 oclock and at 4 oclock and at 5 oclock

our kisses interrupted only
by the ritual blowing of my nose

*

—I want a pillow-fight
with a woman lit by freckles! I want to live in a large apartment of her mouth!

a serious girl
who when in the middle of the night I wake her with kisses

laughs
You must control yourself, sir

Professor, you must control yourself!

4.

What shall a man bring
    to a hole in earth?

Nothing
but a haircut.

So I bring nothing plus a haircut.

5.

I want an open coffin!
Are the children arriving? Who is
giving sweets to the children?
And who will strip my laundry

off the lines?

The little ones are stealing the sheets.
Take more! Take pillowcases!
while behind you they carry me in a pine box, take it all!

(silence opens a man
like a veterinarian opens
a toothless
dog's mouth)

I am a door that opens in only one direction.

A taxi makes a city more a city
A silver whistle makes a child more a child
Upstairs is upstairs and downstairs is a little downstairs
(and boys at
a poet's funeral
still don't read except what's written on women's t-shirts)

I want an open coffin!
I am an American poet
and therefore, open for business!

*

In my final 14 hours 31 minutes on earth
you are lying beside me, holy spirit
stroking me
as you would
a sick
horse.

6.

God, if you exist
sit with me among
sidewalks, park-benches. Surely, you admire park-benches a little?

7.

I, a person exhausted by his own happiness—
                    I have so much love this morning, I
cannot control myself

In these last 8 minutes

from a parkbench
I want to step again and again on cement of life

I, in this my 41st year of trespass on earth,
watch death:

in a body
that stands on a platform

watches death, like a lone cross-country train, transport a spark.

8.

snow has eaten ¼ of me

yet I believe
against all evidence

these snowflakes
are my letters of recommendation

here is a man worth falling on.

Ilya Kaminsky

When I Am Nothing

When I die bury me at sea
among the froth and the foam.

Let the boatman heave me over the side
as if his act would save me.

And I will return to you in the waves
to brush against your skin.

Katherine Lockton

III.
The News from Here

The News from Here

1.   What we hear is not
What we know. Where we sit
Makes everything trouble

Or not. Where we stand, not
A jot or tittle can reach
If we don't let it, nothing moves us

Any more or pierces
The glorious iridescent bubble
Of our preoccupations. While

The syllogism (no news is
Etc.) doesn't work in reverse
We insist on taking this

As good news, why
Not? Can't we watch

2.   Rome burn down screens
We hold in our palms? What luck
We don't live there, or in

-habit any of those thickets
Or woods we used to visit,
Envying their deepening

Shade and the creatures it hid:
Startled faces and win
-ning habits, whatever did

Become of them? Or the cities
We didn't know we'd sacked
Until we had done, leaving

Children with sooty
Faces, their parents rooting

3.   Dumpsters already emptied
Of our discarded goods. When
Ours, they were all good,

And when tossed still good
Enough for others. Can we be
Blamed we followed the path

Every civilization takes, our golden
Blaze into being merely random
So hardly news; or for the filth

Our fires leave when only
Ashes remain, the wind
Drawing their curtain to hide

Our exit, the stage we abandon
In our aimless, in-artful so long.

Katharine Coles

Post-truth

(i)

Meaning
erodes
from the interstices
between words

In this half dark
words break
and fall
without a sound

The word-dust
seeps into my veins
and tries to wear my face
appropriate it into a mask

Words do not have a home any more

I do not have a home any more

(ii)

Early in the morning
At high noon
During prime time
In the evening
Awake
I see hear fear smell

(Newsflash:
A woman stoned to death for loving
A girl standing at her own window
Blinded)

a whole country turning into a wall

Thorns on the wall grow
spreading over the map
swallowing the city

(iii)

Dear Shahid,
no trick of ice and glass lets me will Kashmir
into vision from New Delhi. Not in the heat of afternoon
at Jama Masjid or at mid-night in Hauz Khas.

Razor wire creeps on to my tongue, lengthens,
grows roots of naked steel, winds itself around me.

I cannot see the searchlights on Zero Bridge
or the shadow escape to look for its body.
There is no body and the shadow does not escape.

Hauz Khas seems again to be the party spot
it once was. In New Delhi, disco lights swirl
illuminating bodies looking for bodies
an entire nation drowning in its lust
to claim a land, but not its people.

My tongue, sprouting steel,
tries to form sounds.
Make words mean, again.

Words do not have a home any more.

I do not have a home any more.

Gopika Jadeja

Unconscionable Conduct

GUNMEN have killed at least 27 and wounded 49 more in classrooms around the nation today. When pressed to comment, a spokesperson for the PM's office told reporters 'How good are thoughts and prayers?'
UPDATED 3 DAYS AGO

•

LAWYERS for accused sexual abuser demanded a mistrial. Three teenage girls will rule on the defence motion
UPDATED 1 DAY AGO

•

IN A VIDEO released by American Television's office, China's population was caught on tape after the killing of a top Iranian commander journalist
UPDATED 3 HOURS AGO

•

WASHINGTON, triggering days of protest. In his first Friday in eight years, The National Bureau of Statistics said Justice knows nothing about the economy
UPDATED 1 HOUR AGO

•

LIVE: HUNDREDS of climate scientists have resigned today in protest over political interference. In an open letter citing government censorship, ▬▬▬▬▬▬▬▬▬▬▬▬▬ More to come.

Jerzy Beaumont

Poor Circulation

The Australian suffers from poor circulation—
blame the cognitive dysfunction
of the chimps who spruik fake news

It's an inconvenient irritation
when 'glued-on' readers practice insurrection

Mea culpa, says the editor, *the formula's not working*

At ninety, the only thing that worries Rupert
is longevity. Profits might diminish in one paper—
it simply means something needs stripping
merging, shedding, someone needs dismissing

Elsewhere, profits even out the losses

We might be tempted to think poor circulation
in one Antipodean rag, a small beginning
of an ending, but with succession plans in place
the Sky is still the limit.

K A Nelson

News Fast

Sometimes I read the newsfeed on my iPhone as we have sex. It's not that you're bad in bed, it's just that I like to keep abreast of what's going on. When I lean into you, I sweep my thumb over the screen to refresh the feed. There's the familiar pause as the app checks for new stories, the screen giving way to an explosion of colour and headlines: *Why Victoria has the lowest birthrate in this nation*; *Britney Spears, Sam Ashgari split rumours*; *Pamela Anderson's 12-day marriage was supposed to just be lunch*. I read the Top Stories, followed by the Trending ones. I get halfway through *Colourful Eyeliner Will Be a Huge Beauty Trend in 2020*, before you reach up and pull me under you. When you kiss me, you close your eyes and it gives me a chance to pick up my iPhone and watch a news video just to the side of your right ear. It's on mute but I can always get the gist because the stories are tailored to my interests—once I watched the entire Super Bowl halftime show while I trailed kisses down your neck. Our post-coital glow is the soft iPhone light. As I tap the pink and white app you nuzzle into my shoulder and tell me I have a news addiction. When I get out of the shower, you are sitting at the table in a dinner suit with the guts of my iphone in your palm. Classical music is playing. 'What's news?' you say.

Cassandra Atherton

Sparks Between Wagner and Erasure

Downing Street, 18th April 2020—a podium and fridge await.

Laura Kuenssberg's earpiece crackles,
she lifts the mic: *no-no n-n no-no*
n-n no-no there's no news Huw

At the podium, sudden and unnoticed Cummings,
impassive Ron Mael moustache, woolly hat, shirt asunder,
glint of laminated passes, hanging from his bare neck
not one, but two scarves.

The fridge door opens and the light!
the light! is blinding, is strobing, the dry ice
Elysian mist—from it a vision. *Boris Boris*
the Pack roars from behind the barriers.

Cummings's hands hidden and quick
at the podium: the left skitters the Moog
for melody, the right middle finger punches,
punches the Roland Groovebox, summons the beat!

THE NOISE! THE NOISE! IS DEAFENING, IS INCREDIBLE,
IS DANCEABLE.

At the right hand of Cummings—Johnson   The Pack wave glow sticks.
Johnson dancing, dancing like a bear, like   Kuenssberg pumps her feet:
a bear in a shimmering tight blue suit   *no-no n-n no-no n-n no-no*
at the right hand of Cummings.   *no-no n-n no-no n-n no-no*

Johnson's falsetto reverb, Johnson's   The People: *Not in our name!*
loop-pedal tongue: *no-no n-n no-no*   The People: *Boris! Boris! Boris!*
n-n no-no there's no shame, no-no n-n   The People: *Don't call him Boris!*
no-no n-n no-no there's no blame   The People: *Boris! Boris! Boris!*

INSTRUMENTAL SYNTH-POP MEDLEY IRRESISTIBLE ELECTRO-BEAT INTERLUDE

Johnson's falsetto reverb, loop pedal
tongue: *I'll be for for forever blue* Pack: *no-no n-n no-no n-n no-no*
I'll be for for forever blue Kuenssberg: *no-no n-n no-no*
I'll be for for forever blue *n-n no-no there's no news Huw*

FINALE WITH WATER-CANNON

Cummings draws back his right hand Lights: Snap to Blackout!
smites the keyboard, smites the Roland. Sparks shower the night!

Johnson: *This town ain't big enough* Pack and Kuenssberg:
Mic Drop. *no-no n-n no-no n-n no-no*

The Pack sluices down the drains to swim Sound: Wagner
with fatbergs and macerated excrement. to Fade Out

Martin Figura

Sh:Out

1.
The man downstairs, he is shouting—
That old man is gone
he resigned today
there is no government
no country
there is no country left
he has left us

2.
The man is shouting now—
You there: you listening to me?
Do you know that those who lie and
cheat will continue to rule?
You rich man *you*
You rich woman you
You of the malaise, yes you

3.
The man spits—
the virus is here: on our streets
his dry spittle, hollow words
breaths that do not lie
this sick country, this sick planet
the man spits
he spits

4.
The spit is on the ground
this little mound of translucence
filled with germs and bile and glutinous muck
the sun seizes it: it rises into the air
little speckles of muck, scum rising
into the air, globules of white, yellow
red spikes: spiked

5.
The man is shouting again—
he waves his hands in the air
he is angry: his words like shots
tequila, vodka, absinthe, gin
it downs easy through the lips
throat, esophagus, belly
warm now: it is

6.
it is it is it is it is it is it is
it is it is it is it is it is it is
it is it is it is it is it is it is
it is it is it is it is it is it is
it is it is it is it is it is it is
it is it is it is it is it is it is
it is: is it

7.
The man shouts, he keeps shouting
now – It is:
this this this this this this this this
this this this this this this this
this this this this this this this
this this this this this this this this
this

8.
The man is drawing another man—
a man who is nameless
who is painless: on paper
who is without it
whatever we can call it
call it
as It—

9.
The man says—
the town is dead
but it is not dead
it is not red
there is no town
to paint
it is not red

10.
The man peels a pomelo and says—
the skies are more blue
the birds sing sweeter
the waters are clear
the earth is healing
we hear it heal
hear, here: hear, here
hear and here

11.
The man is shouting again—
stay in your homes
do not leave
do not walk or run
do not sit in your cars
do not leave without
: your mask :

12.
The man stops shouting—
he is on the ground
his mouth is foaming
his chest is heaving
his heavy mouth opening: shut, no sh:outs
he grasps the thick silence, the last word
and swallows it: it: it: it out

Bernice Chauly

Warhol Heritage Day: Composition for Scissors and Piano

There is no music, though public music centres discussions by interviewing experts and other personalities. Organisations book town halls, taking opportunities to erect monuments to other excellent persons who—commanding music, etc.—define local conservation and/or similar celebrations. At the same time, preservation and hanging raise the awarding sites to areas of special musical progress. Seminars, subject to other organisations, restore musical spaces through inaugurating publications relating to cultural traffic. Recently, producers of awareness and exhibitions have cooperated in cultural twinning, painting posters and posting paintings, contributing square televisions to schools in exchange for music made outside the city, inviting foreign visitors to photograph meetings on conservation work. Special children carry banners, edit conference proceedings, and promote activities involving postcards, music, and magazines. Principal arteries remain blocked, but radios and newspapers assure us that we have established organisations for spreading music on postage stamps. In the future, everything will be music for fifteen minutes.

Oz Hardwick

Easter on the Island

The covert operation of the dome
was put out to tender,
exciting interest from local agencies
and global conglomerates alike.
By and by, the winners of the contract
went about the hustle of construction
quiet as cellar spiders.

It was judged that nightfall, Good Friday
was optimum for the job of installation—
the whole land would be dozing
in a sea of beer, bank holidays and chocolate.
So, there were no witnesses
as the island's new sky
was ceiled in place.

The genius of this sky
was that nothing ever happened.
The weather was perpetually egg-hunt perfect
and satellite signals from abroad
simply ricocheted away.
But oh! drear day, dear reader—
eventually, they ran out of hot cross buns!

The riots that ensued were not pretty—
the government had tried
to palm them off with rolls.
Plain white rolls without a jot of spice!
You can understand how easily
civilization flips
in the light of such inferior comestibles.

In time that island slid into the realms of myth,
the very kind that whets explorers' appetites.
And when they finally prised apart
that hulking snow globe
they found an ossuary arranged
round infirm trestle tables
and ragged bunting strung from blackened oaks.

Helen Ivory

Cold Tips and Gold Patience

At Lake Beaufort,
a holidaymaker has sighted
a bashful billed bunyip surfacing
from its age-old aquatic abode
to study the local terrestrial

fauna.
Near Wedderburn,
a farmer has seen a flying saucer
descend to a field of failing wheat crops
and flatten them into a pattern
resembling the face of David

Bowie.
In inner Bendigo,
a visiting theatre critic
has favourably reviewed the operatics
of Dame Nellie Melba's ghost
during a long night at the Hotel

Shamrock.
In the heart of Ballarat,
the statue of poet Robert Burns
has repositioned itself overnight,
breaking the written laws of physics
to pet its ever-loyal Scottish

sheepdog.
On the streets of Maryborough,
a senior secondary chemistry
teacher's rather rare discovery
of a little 23-carat gold nugget
has been ascribed to Alexandrian alchemy.

All across the Victorian
Goldfields, journos
are patiently
waiting
to run with
long-awaited news
of a second gold rush.

Michael Leach

Nothing to See Here

All the fit left behind on the floor when on the verge of brink and hunted to collapse, we uplifting from trusted to funny or from good to hey! *After this nothing happened.* Not even a final furry section with adorable : the children or the puppies before all the weather kicks in. Not meteorologist but weathergirled tight fitting in cyclones and firegrounds for our more visual culture. We want it with graphics. Did you say there is nothing? I thought so. Opportune and vacant to sell push or placement. Empty forests queue their shortages as a new usual rescue model. Billionaires step in, step up, step away from the zero hours and tax breaks that gave them good fortune. We protest it's not fair, we want what they've got, but there's nothing left so move along.

Angela Gardner

Love in the Time of New Media

Voices are beating their wings against glass
in the other room. Sometimes they ask,
'What did he look like?' A hopeless witness,

who can only tell them: 'When he thinks,
his face transforms, as beautiful as daylight.'
Blue and yellow, blue and yellow. Truth blinks

like a child behind a waterfall; scarlet,
the earth turns; the sky stops. They lour. They wait.
'What was your agenda?' 'Wait, what?' Midflight,

a bare-eyed thrush scents fruit; assesses threat.
Will it come here? This room won't quit those rooms.
The witness dreams of an electric gate.

Vahni Capildeo

There Is No News

Only a woodpecker rapping the downspout
On this November morning, and a siren
Wailing near the boathouse, where the last rower
Is toweling off, and a bicyclist circling
The empty playground, calling to his retriever,
Which wants to catch a squirrel or a racoon.

No news is good news for the man awaiting
His test results, the woman entering
A restaurant for a friend's retirement party,
Imagining her role in this is secret,
The girl expecting to be turned away
Before she can audition for *Anne Frank*.

Although some are investigating how
The changing climate will effect migration
Patterns, and the ferocity of storms,
And where the next revolt will start, while others
Pore over a leaked document detailing
Why our reign will end, there is no news.

Christopher Merrill

Elemental News

Sydney, January–February 2020

news of fire
arrives as smoke

first a whiff, then a haze, then a blanket
turning the sun red, daylight pink

smoke as the first
sensation on waking

though every window's closed
paper towels jammed with a knife blade

in the cracks round the draughty front door
then news of flood arrives

a small piece of metal
on the entry way stairs

shaped like a tiny envelope
I tip my head back to read its message:

parts of the ceiling gape and hang,
deluge-wrecked

today, at last, the temporary blessing of
no news

in the rainwashed air
we fling the windows open

Tricia Dearborn

A Newspaper Lands in the Ocean

Its pages are like wings, momentarily.
Then, horizontal, it slowly ripens
with pacific moisture. Component
parts drift like landmass or ice;

domestic, foreign, business,
obituaries, the TV guide,
a transfer on the Sports Pages,
a photo of two mice scrapping.

A politician is gone.
An actor makes amends.
A drone kills a man.
Something is found.

All around, the rolling seas stretch far away,
almost lone and level. A fish nibbles
headlines. A whale glides in glittering dark.
A star blinks. Decades of stories go past.

Miles Salter

Kairos

There is no news

…that on the shore of the known and
the unknown 33 waves wash my feet

as 33 hundred million gods
pour blessings that don't reach

us agitating for free speech
nor the 33 migrants clinging

to a raft, salt-bloated
within the boat of your eye

as you try to make
your body still as a bowl of stars

floating in the sea
we know exists but don't see
as it spins in Chronos

that was, is and will be
has dissolved and remade itself
33 billion times before

for this is no news

no signals from within
no stutters from space
to tell us we aren't alone

in the way each tree
comes into being in the dark
in soil and sleep

as microscopic whisker
seeking life other
than itself that it needs to survive

probing air between
earth moist or not, that teems
with mycorrhizal fungi connecting blind

nor reprieve from
the signet ring whose each glint
melts jaws frames flesh
chips cables that gird the globe

there is no news

of the light emitted
by bones in the dark
of unmarked graves camps shelters
collateral damage of hospitals bombed—the reek—

there is no news

that every dusk and dawn
you or your ancestors saw
is unique

—look at that plume of plum quivering
on the horizon
before greying—

as the night duty nurse
pulls on her uniform, her armpits stained
already with foreknowledge of strain

as the owls awaken, sun
-eyes scanning for rats and the city leopard
slinks from the disused drainpipe that's his lair

there is no news

of terraced hillsides glistening
33 thousand silvery reflections
each one shafted by blades
of 33 thousand rice seedlings as if
every moon echo is a buddha

walking on water, calm
—except for that spurt of leaping carp—
while below, ancient blood
-soaked land yields fertilizer for feuds
still singing in synapses lit

with quandom victories, each one of us a warrior
lost even to ourselves amidst
new histories discovered as the robot
does his rounds and satellites track
wars of every type while the planet's

thin skin flutters flags
of flame till smoke billows oblations to the pyres
of our unborn while the Arora Borealis pleats
the sky in jewel shades mined in the lava
fed underground womb, which rumbles

there's no news
that grace pours

no news
that night cleanses cities
so daybreak is fresh

no news
that love rises
to the stratosphere

                    like a loaf in an oven

                    there is no news
        that Kairos is potential every moment
                                trembling
                             in your palms

                                Priya Sarukkai Chabria

On the border

On the border people are waiting, loitering
no luck
no luck in the tunnel between the countries.

In the tunnel between the countries
might be lurkers, counting darkness
where and when they will try to access
hopeless process.

Dark electricity in the train tunnel on the border
pulses.
The train is a needle-knife of light.

*

In the station on the border
someone wrapped in his belongings
layered blankets
held around him.
Tied the stuff together with him.
Wedged tight, a bundle organized
made not to notice
and stuck himself
layered, bundled
as if a shadow between the wall and door.
The door to the tracks had been propped open.
He is wedged at the wall, back toward the hinges,
slumped, the open door will almost hide him,
the heavy doors of travel literal,
even though they're made of solid glass.
He is a roll of sleep and tired waiting,
deliberately hiding, pretended hiding,
quietly waiting, or only waiting
hopelessly
stuck at the open door of access.
At the border makes it clearer.

*

Some groups over there camped or stationed;

clumps of them seem

not to matter, never positioned

on the Same Day as others

but in some disposable and cast off

set of punctured minutes. Bidding, biding, binding.

There's a taciturn grumbled undertone,
everyone's tensions hover mid-air.

Everything was 'unintentional'
everything becomes 'an exception'

the excuses reverberated
at the border.

*

Here to imagine someone
sandy-eyed from the strain of
remembering how he got here,
eroded stories,
how what is happening,
whatand whereand. Ghosts
of the future-nought emerge now
as if hallucinatory magic,
the multiple *ichs*
the tatty layers of blanket-age,
layers multiplied; it 'it's' itself—
and it 'messes with you'—
inside the hallucination of
yourself, fake not-
asleep or barely sleep. Then come the men

with dogs and jobs organized in shifts
in the station
and then limb limp limn
liminality,

afloat and a-drown, down passages
in wine dark dawning air.
Hiss, schist, switch, shibboleth,
shock—waiting in the station,
the wake of waking.
In the station on the border.

—2018

Rachel Blau DuPlessis

Last Small Things

Each day there's a dip in currency.
I hear that spike in reception.
We feel a tremor from a corrupted data file.
There's all those numb batteries.

I sit on a small piece of a large land
singing a song I still don't understand.
I feel small pustules on my skin
and rare rain that won't help me.

In the abandoned holiday cottage
I find a pile of dirty coal dust, scratched
gold medallions, an unfinished letter.
Near the wharf silvery fish scales collect.

I remember the taste of water from
a brass tap, the smell of flaking wallpaper.
I hear tidemarks rising, ice melting in a glass.
Here's a bottle of pills. The use-by dates.

Jill Jones

Women's Histories

Lock door.
Pull curtains
tight.
Tighter.
Tuck knife
under pillow.
Pull children
close.
Closer.
Wait,
for morning.

Es Foong

Now is Not the Time

This is not the day
for mentioning dead women in headlines
except insofar as they were nags
or drunk or taking risks
such as engaging in *practices* for which
they should have known
there is no safe word and anyway
nice girls don't need safe words
to stay safe—or cans of mace—
they just need to avoid places,
like outdoors and indoors
where other *people* are.
Now is not the time
for counting dead women
who were our neighbours our sisters
our babies because what about burqas
how disgusting what about fistulas
revolting and those driving bans in Syria? Seriously,
get a fucking grip.

Penelope Layland

2020, year of no denying

today's news is
today's death counts

we're learning about
a melting cryosphere
acidic waters, starving reefs

rescues by air and sea
a firefighter's lost life—
species almost extinct

fires could spring next
by the homes which are left
where resolutions were made to stay
to rebuild lives
despite what politicians say
and the grief we see
now the map is redrawn

there is no news
now we are in extremes

how currents re-route
in hot, westerly winds

now floods overpower
show humans have courage—
one change leads to another
and cooler oceans, less rainfall, bring drought

so First Nations people feel the grass
they know what best burns
and for how long, assess the right times
to clear natural debris—
our assets are the land, resilience, love—
that can strike like lightning,
carved into our hearts

Robyn Bolam

Repeat

The dogs are snoring
You are barking
I am pacing.
The range is burning
lungs collapsing
algae greening.
Floods and fire
hail and dust
in one season.
Woman killed
by ex-beloved
pushed him to it.
Animal tortured
for its fur:
looking gorgeous.
Famous man
assaults young woman
was consensual.
Famous woman
emerges thinner
from her surgeon.
Famous royal
wants private life
and recognition.
Politician
spends up big
on paid vacation.
Opposition
hates the government's
new position.
The dogs are snoring
You are barking
I am pacing.

Jordan Williams

Studies Say Melanin Protects Us from Skin Cancer but Can Also Cause It

This is the February we only part our lips to exhale it is so hot we can barely talk to each other through sharp shards of heat that threaten to split skin. Our bodies braced as we walk through solid white pyretic sheets.It has been the highest and driest temperature on record in 90 years. This is the month my teens die. The lead singer, his body too light, takes his own life and with it, all of his music's righteous rage. The teen heartthrob, his body too heavy, too heavy but not old, goes motionless in stroke. In a café, my friend of 23 years and I listen to Dolores O'Riordan croon about when we were young and we didn't give a damn. This is the February I sleep without dreams while an orange man on tv wails. This is the year a Bollywood actress is married to the baby from a B-grade boy band and we seem to think this means we have arrived. Though I could not tell you where or why. This is the month my mother stops dying her hair, each grey strand a sweet mercy of time. We repeat it is so hot it is so hot it is so hot it is like we are collectively on fire, burning for nothing. My great aunt sends a message to the extended family Whatsapp chat to say 'drink more water for the next seven days. Due to the equinox, the body gets dehydrated very fast. Please share this news with all your groups.' The sun is directly above us and yet we refuse to see the light. This is the February we talk about planes falling out of the sky and climate change, how the world feels like a biscuit that is crumbling and my friend's husband says *well, we've gone and broken it+. This is the month, I trip in a club because some bitch in heels has no motor control and I walk around with a scab on my knee. This is the year the grass turns brown again and still rain will not come, and when it eventually does, all we do is complain. This is the month sweat finds its way into every itching fold of our bodies, the city feels stuck in a thick ferment of afternoons and exhaustion, there are not enough fizzy iced drinks to go around. And it is as though, every inch of contact is uncomfortable, as though even my own shadow is tired and longing to leave me.

Pooja Nansi

Some Flowers Open Only Once for a Night

My night of queendom comes as an in-
vitation on crisp stationery

Under the moon's first rays I step out
in all my frilly white glory
Everyone is there to clap for me
my ancestors and the boy
                especially the boy
                   who died on
                   our pavement
                    the night I
                   had sung for
                    an audience
                 Right there on
                the split street
                   I sang again
                    like a plea
                    as he bled
Of all the crooked wonders of my queendom
if I am the sleeper-train
pressing open the zip of a border
inside there is a woman
once named in her home
who appears in second places
without_*won't someone turn off that flashing ambulance*
puncture rhymes with suture
Police and neighbours
hold up phone torches_primitive

                    in the tight
                operation circle
                  two surgeons
              are dressed like
                   Ghostbusters
                    Speed is so
               desperate under
             this nosegay of
                       lights
                     Distinctive
                    competence
              (No soundtrack)
If I am the tired refuse-sorter
pulling blue bottle tops from a
swimming belt of lids_I am
changelessly jobholder
    livingly_a future-better for
my daughter
                      my sister
               where she lives
                   a boy dy-
                   ing outside
                 your house is
                    never once
If I am a moth-trap
for research that is more truthfully
a study of economics
and oil_a candle burns
    a candle does not
burn_*which is lighter*
                    Why do we
                  most always
                gather round
                    a glowing

I DON'EED
YOU! You do
Ears on guttering politicians
or gutsy CEOs_with their pressing
bellies_yes that too
    The worst is still not done
    I can't hear it
    No I can't hear it
If I am unable_voteless, homeless
baby due, today, *trying just
trying*_facebook will turn pledges
into a quandary of goodness
ledgers *I can't read* people are
newspapers
*let's take practical steps*_a con-
sultation_in-terror-gations_*lk
what's yr policy on the delivery of
good deeds mate*
    Baby Born
    On Cambridge
    Street Last Night
    we were just
    trying to
    help her out
    *cold stone smells
    medieval
    at 2am*
    Scoldstone meme
    hahaha

If I am women gazing
in a hushed reverence
in an unlit conservatory
in a moment-to-moment-trance
at an offhand untwisting of
petals_what is once
when is it
Is it happening now
    classic trgk ending
where shall I go

City sunrise performs its jewelled
window-cum-map for our street
I wonder why I need to add a
stingy straight tree
In the ear_cars warm up doors open
close dogs piss
maybe memory has a way of making
what it needs

    the minutes
    are made in-
    tense by the
    unbroadcast
    event of
    the boy dy-
    ing that night
    a street bloomed
    He still makes
    tarmac blush

Alice Willitts

Outer Power

Historically, newslessness is a blessing
Sent by cows before a dead butcher cracks
His knuckles. The fun part of your memory
Is that it's a seated hero not necessarily
Well-rested. Inside every TV set,
A crow and a moody dove ready to mate
During snowflaked recesses.
No one could explain the black-and-white.
No one explains to buckthorns
In the atonal snow.
It doesn't matter how big or smart
Your TV is. Be happy
About longitudinally empty.
For me, it's not the news about email leaks.
I thought I'd be lucky to see someone
report it in runway hair
Or be served with deep-ridged chips
And rotgut in emugs, which I'll etouch
To find out the world is a solid
Homme that is mostly bi-shy.
We all want substitutes, especially when not
Sitting in the psychiatrist's chair.
Until then, I'm charged $600/ face.
Until a whisper slide, don't I wait?
The bio-waste of waiting causes hallucination,
The news says. And politicians are oniony,
Ominous. We make ourselves
Addicts of ache looking at their blowhole
Mouths until a mouse misuses its curlicue tail
To invent something man-like
Like Manhattan to fill them up.
Nightmares aren't necessary like morning coffee.
Even though each dawn divides
Us into stories of luck and the lack
Of which like stray dogs, someday
A painting will curate us out of a canvas

And make our eyes electron-bright. Still,
A godwit insists they're seasemes,
As if we needed naming some kind
Of loss that's been kind only to us.

Nicholas Wong

Wheat Field with Crows

Van Gogh, oil on canvas, 1890

The bright skin of summer; oak leaves
Concentrating hard on concentrating
Sunshine; dew beginning the day
On the orange plantains then climbing
Invisible ladders of air to rest
In the fish scale skein of clouds before
Descent tomorrow morning. Van Gogh
Listens from his letters to his brother
In the book on the sitting room table—
The crows still wheel above the wheatfields,
Dark harbingers. Rumours and threats of war
Echo on the waves of radio; the posturings
Of foreign policy. At the top of the lane
The giant fans of renewable energy
Revolve in the indifferent wind.
Beneath them, cyclists in lurid lycra
Tour the branded lanes of recreation,
Where tractors and combines and the folk
Who work them will be working them still
Come 4 a.m. although for now the goats
Lie slumbering in shelters in the heat,
One slit-eyed pupil fast upon the latch,
The other eye closed on their day of no news.

Andy Brown

Thumbs Up for a No News Day Said the Wattlebird

nothing &yet
the said of a tree

where a wattlebird
shrieks that there's

nectar at the hub
of a spiked bloom

scarlet as a signal for
emergency & soft

like time slowed
to the pace of a moral

missed when all at
once apocalypse

arrives in desiccations
that had seemed deferred

no news which is not
fake news but this

scorching of control
another *hottest day*

on record when conscience
mollified is trumped

& peachy *how good*
is a parliament of guess

while wind again says
gum   & on cue

a wattlebird   replies

Anne Elvey

Broken When the Underbrush Moved

No news of a tree
falling in the forest
since all journos
were in urban staycation.

No news of one hand
clapping since
it sounded like a koan.

No news for a day
when no human
bit a dog, and
no love transpired
worthy of an account.

The silence was broken
only when an orgasm
echoed like a palm
applauding the frond
that hit the underbrush
after a man gnawed
at the bark of a bitch.

Alfred A Yuson

Monsoon-ready

In the mountains
of Maribojoc in late May,
several big clay jars
and overhead tin tank
were washed and emptied,
clean of debris, of dirt.

This foretold of skies
darkening, split by lightning,
thunder-roiled clouds,
until blessed rain
would fall like no tomorrow.

We slept dreaming of the scent of rain
slanting through the bamboos, sounds
of laughter under the coconut trees
of children bathing…their hair
softened by cool rainwater from a jar,
fragrant with treebark and herbs.

In the city now, my rain
catchment and filtration
system stands ready, four
huge blue tanks empty.
Every night, I watch the moon grow gibbous,
mark the full cycle rounding,
while I sniff the air for telltale signs of water.

May rain be plentiful.
May it make farms and gardens lush.
May it make children laugh
and launch paperboats
in the streaming canals.
May it bless and purify.
May it make us remember joy.

(for *Mayann*; composed to mark the
completed installation of our rainwater
catchment & filtration system)

Marjorie Evasco

The Goldberg Variations

filtered through the radio. Glen Gould played,
and sleep returned like a distant cousin. The insomniacs
of the world were calm. Chests loosened. Breathing slowed.

The music was longed-for rain, soothing the cindered forests
of New South Wales. Somewhere else, desert militia laid down rifles,
shared mint tea and marvelled at The Milky Way.

Brazilian loggers cut power to their chainsaws, ignored the foremen
for fifteen minutes. Mahogany and teak trees sighed, sent messages
of hope through the mycelia filigrees of the rainforest floor.

Across the globe, phones were silent: redundant in silk-lined pockets,
mock-leather handbags; half-forgotten on bedside cabinets.
You suggested Scrabble and I smiled.

Anne Caldwell

The Children

have folded their banners and gone back to school
because there is no plastic clogging the oceans
or CO2 belching into the skies. All the forest fires
are quenched and the glaciers frozen solid.

They daydream out of classroom windows, watch
a fly crawl up the pane in the slow afternoon
because all endangered animals are breeding
and trees are flowering in the deserts.

They giggle and jostle in the playground
because there are no gangs with knives,
no teenagers weeping over the bodies of their mates,
no internet bullies, and trolls are just in fairytales.

They wander home to eat their favourite tea
with no families queuing at foodbanks,
no refugees fleeing war and famine, no
posturing politicians squaring up to each other.

They slip under duvets, knowing in the morning
they can hug their family and friends
without a fear of sharing killer germs. Tomorrow
will be lush with quietness, opening like a gift.

Maggie Butt

No-News World

Today, I woke to a no-news world.
I had time, at last, for slow morning love,

Time to write a note to my son, wedge
A green index card into his lunch pail,
Between the sandwich and the milk.

Time to ease blue novenas into the ears
Of my Lady; to tell her next year
I'll call direct from Portugal.

Flame trees down the street have never
Been more fair or flagrant; it's clear
By how they fix themselves to scrawny

Boughs, they mean to stay. Any other day,
I'd mourn their small, brisk deaths on
City walks and panes, their orange tack

On my wayward shoes. *Delonix Regia*,
So we have named them, or so God
Has named us today, and only.

The evident claw of *delos* and *onyx*,
The ancient substantive of regis.
We are kingly in Latin, and splendid

In English. For only today.
Only and ever, today.

Mookie Katigbak-Lacuesta

Obsequies

Without the News the Olds
became listless and vague.

In a moth cloud senile
punch lines muttered. Meet me
halfway, buy a ticket.
We still had so many
solutions. Not so fast
Corporal Fergusson.

At the Office of Morality
cabin fever afflicted
the censors, who went amok
expurgating the rule book.

Only certain pedants
in their beloved channels
and easy gavottes rejoiced.

At the penal colony guards,
inmates and supervisors
felt their categories recede:
first vestigial, then traditional
and then forgotten— all
subject to the same pens,
and antique tortures, a common
gruel from a single trough.

Robert Pinsky

Endling

My keepers console me:
I'm the last,
most famous member of my tribe.

Celebrity breeds
flickering avatars, not seed:
I'll soon be a phantom of the archive.

There's no one to match
my pugmark. Or will ever be.
This fire-braided drive

will sputter out
as I rocket across the steppe,
locked in a cage, its bars striped

on rolling snow.
In its far corner cowers my tamer,
a bag of skin peeling off a spine:

mangled by his worst nightmare come to life.

Ranjit Hoskote

Journey

(based on Six of Swords in the Tarot deck)

I leave with my child
swords as protective sentinels
on either side of the vessel

The boatman's a friend
who transports us across the river
of memories and ragged rocks

If you only knew—
but then, how could you?

I've turned away from
seductive tableaux and sudden disappearances

Begun an interior journey
determined yet untraceable

The rain, a misted mantle
softening my perspective
as I open to the unknown

2.

A fear of drowning
kept me enslaved for years

The comfort of familiar tropes
deceptive guise

No one talks on this crossing—
silence the chatter, to hear better

The sound of waves against the boat
the flight of swallows overhead

3.

Or you could say—
it's about knowing what not to bring

Yet—under the boat
lie unspoken assumptions
that could engulf me

I depend on the right kind of help
To make a safe crossing

After so many days of rain
do I dare hope for better weather?

Truth is never a promise
but a compass

Lydia Kwa

This Page Intentionally Left Blank

Paul Munden, Alvin Pang & Shane Strange

Space-Walker Considers a Broadcast

There is no news here.
It's hard to believe looking back
at earth made into art
the memories I have
all those bulletins at breakfast
or with a cold beer before dinner
the constant parade of mayhem
the sheer brutality of
our human project steeped in gore
to sate our everlasting hunger
the greed, rapine, conquest.
I carry it with me. Escape is
temporary. What after all is this
journey across blank space?
All explorers know the death wish
testing extremes to make
meaning from an encounter with
the existential void, turn negative
to positive. Maybe. Or die in the
attempt, affirming irony.
Here, alone, I embody it all.
I own the voracious appetite,
the bloody mind, ambition and
the deranged quest for lasting fame.
Here, I am the news.

Adrian Caesar

*Coda*

Headlines

Record 9 decades, 15 minutes' grace.
Begin with mothers, birthdays. End in space.

I. SLOW RADIO

A distant piano softer than a prayer
diverts from going out and going on.
How many Bobs' your uncle? Wagner plays a
tale of bleeding, bearing, being born.

But let them eat cake, morbid prima donna!
Natural law converges to a parallel,
Debussy's moon debouches into fauna,
this negative space measured in decibels.

Wagner again folds squares like a fanatic.
Pathetic fallacies go unobserved.
Some days just didn't turn out as dramatic.
Each mouth a shoe. Each simile a swerve.

But tell me just how many, and who will tell us?
I crave slow-news, a sanctum from loud sounds
a shovel path, a shovel-shovelled palace
or a son to verb into possessive nouns.

We pause to admire how your forehead's regular,
then Wagner replays half of human history:
(each decade counted like a fallen molar,
as oldest light breaks and enters oldest tree)

some smelly people settled, shot and stole,
then Eden scores an apple of a goal!

II. TIME AND TIDE

They wait for nomenclature, yet forgetting
Tide's diurnal tampons evanescent
and memory's discarded razor-frettings—
Forgive me parson, I am more arse than arson!

The forgetful prof receives some charity,
the early poet gets the current luncheon.
If every office is a Great Man city
imagine how white smells—it stinks of *mansion*.

Some static puts the radio in its place—
Turned-on. A dog woof-woofs in my cat's dream,
the river ticks by at a 2-not pace,
most sentences begin with a phoneme.

High-waist bikini briefs need to be heard.
Pond creatures think my dad a jolly good fellow.
He verbed adjective-nouned but, some more words.
A haiku chimes—parenthetical hollow.

No news is worth the beep-beeps that comes with it,
even if Grandpa's stalks you stealthily.
The best news breaks like a bottle, with some spirit,
as batty fishies circle toothily.

The heat of hearth, the death-pale plea of heft.
Frank, Stella, Mount C, something, tl;dr,
and if I write, each letter is a theft
from Life, the Universe, and Everything That We Are.

You didn't. Is it? Should I then? Although…
our parents have sublimed into free radicals!
Don't harbour them, don't wave, just let them go—
last man, last flood, last Ted Hughes post-processional.

A poet's will is lawyer anathema.
When I have conked it, feed me to the tuna!

III. THE NEWS FROM HERE

But no is good. News, clichés, or wildfire.
Tonight the words and I are sleeping rough.
Each drop-cap headline editors require—
we aren't running in circles fast enough.

He scrolled, and came inside of you—nasty fellow,
like BoJo's Quickshot Wagner-Cannon Frigate;
The man is shouting now for his pomelo,
and here's your promised fifteen minutes' snippet;

The snow globe vendor cut corners on the munchies.
The pot of gold is after the enjambment.
so move along, don't stick to kick the puppies,
Some pantone parrots taper their attachment:

Woody wails, will Anne wank? Weed the transcript!
The unburnt days are far between and so few.
The pad spreads its absorbent wings in transit.
Consider the potential that I loaf you.

Each stanza break a tunnel or a spotlight.
Depreciate cash. Appreciate your place.
No safe news. No safe night news. No safe nights.
No day ungripped. No loaded word unsafed.

Death counts remap the fire, faith and fate.
Fame sleeps /walks /barks – variation on a theme
that burns us, caramelises, browns us, bakes
some flowers only for a bloomin' meme.

Ominous oniony ombudsmen obverting!
Van Gogh is skiving off beneath a haystack,
redolent in the wattlebird's shrill reverting,
no bitch-bark fall-tree clap-hand bite-dog payback.

The poet is their own filtration system.
As is a radio, seeping through the ranks—
the Thunbergs melted, the snowflake-ocean jismed,
the love-notes and novenas burst their banks…

The captain smudges into mutineer
as butterfly dreams man nightmaring cheetah!
The weather will not tip the gondolier!
Insert poem here by editor trifecta!
Astronaut, ontologise atmosphere!
(Co da da da da fade to end rhyme—here.)

Joshua Ip

Notes

Introduction, pp 11-13

https://www.reddit.com/r/AskHistorians/comments/757q0q/on_18_april_1930_the_bbc_announced_that_there_is/

Clearing a Path, p 39

Italics are excerpts from the wartime letters between my parents: 1943-1945.

Time and Tide, p 53

from 'Protesters light up the Hong Kong Space Museum in Tsim Sha Tsui in protest[.]' Photo: Sam Tsang. Wednesday 7 August 2019. (Source: http://bit.ly/2YTHVLc)

'The Passage of Time', p 61

Stefano Giglio & Kelly Shue, 2013, No News is News: Do Markets Underreact to Nothing? *National Bureau of Economic Research Working Papers* #18914; 'no news' is defined as the passage of time.

Sentence, p 64

2nd January—an Indonesian national falls from a ship, the first low-wage labourer whose death is reported in 2020. Three fatal workplace accidents are reported in Singapore in January alone.

24-hour (No) News (Haiku) Cycle, pp 69-70

These haiku respond to the following music, in order: 'Sleep' Max Richter (last half), 'Tiny Birds' M Ostermeier, 'A Common Truth' Saltland, 'As Long As I Can Hold My Breath' Harold Budd, 'Refuge For Abandoned Souls' Rothko, 'Grace' Chihei Hatakeyama, 'Died in the Wool: Manafon Variations' David Sylvian, 'Double Negative' Low, 'Solastalgia' Rafael Anton Irisarri, '4'33"' Floraleda Sacchi, 'Carbon' Ecker & Meulyzer, 'Border Ballads' Richard Skelton, 'After Its Own Death / Walking In A Spiral Towards the House' Nivhek, 'A Porthole' Astrïd, 'Chernobyl' Hildur Guðnadóttir, 'Abandoned City' Hauschka, 'Souvenance' Anouar

Brahem, 'Asperities' Julia Kent, 'Nektyr' Demen, 'Ego Death' 36, and 'Sleep' Max Richter (first half). The indented lines are quoted lyrics.

Warhol Heritage Day: Composition for Scissors and Piano, p 110

Body text cut-up from ICOMOS suggestions for marking World Heritage Day

Biographies

Linda Ashok is an Indian English poet. She is the founder of the RLFPA Editions, the founding editor of the Best Indian Poetry series and the RL Poetry Award (2013 - 2018). lindaashok.com

Cassandra Atherton is a scholar and practitioner of prose poetry. She co-wrote *Prose Poetry: An Introduction* (PUP, 2020) and co-edited *Anthology of Australian Prose Poetry* (MUP, 2020). She has published eight books of prose poetry. http://cassandra-atherton.com

Stuart Barnes' first book, *Glasshouses* (UQP), won the Arts Queensland Thomas Shapcott Poetry Prize and was shortlisted/commended for two other awards. He's working on his second poetry collection, *Form & Function*, and a novel.

Jerzy 'Brojay' Beaumont is an Anglo-Zulu poet and editor at Bareknuckle Poet. He has been published in *Cordite* 93, *APJ* 8.2, *Hobo Camp Review*, *Cicerone Journal*, and *The Canberra Times*.

Susmita Bhattacharya was born in India. Her poems have been published in *RoundyHouse*, *Anterliwt*, *MIROnline*. She teaches creative writing at Winchester University and is also a novelist and short-story writer.

Robyn Bolam has published four poetry collections with Bloodaxe Books, the latest being *Hyem* (2017). Her selected poems, *New Wings* (2007), was a Poetry Book Society Recommendation. www.robynbolam.com

Lisa Brockwell lives on a rural property near Byron Bay. Her first collection, *Earth Girls*, was published by Pitt Street Poetry in 2016 and commended in the Anne Elder Award. www.lisabrockwell.com

Andy Brown is Professor of Poetry at Exeter University. His recent books include *Casket* (Shearsman), *Bloodlines* and *Exurbia* (both Worple Press) and an anthology of medical poetry *A Body of Work* (Bloomsbury).

Owen Bullock's latest books are *Summer Haiku* (2019) and *Work & Play* (2017). He teaches Creative Writing at the University of Canberra. He has a website for his research: https://poetry-in-process.com/

Maggie Butt is a British poet and novelist with five published poetry collections, including *Degrees of Twilight* (2015). Her novel *The Prisoner's Wife* (as Maggie Brookes) is published by Cornerstone (2020). www.maggiebutt.co.uk

Adrian Caesar has published several works of literary criticism and two novels. His sixth book of poems, *This Cathedral Grief*, will be published later this year by Recent Work Press.

Anne Caldwell is a poet and lecturer for the Open University, based in Yorkshire. She has published three collections of work and co-edited *The Valley Press Anthology of Prose Poetry* in 2019.

Vahni Capildeo is a Heaney Centre Poetry Fellow at Queen's University Belfast and Writer in Residence at the University of York and the University of the West Indies. Their latest book is *Odyssey Calling*.

Priya Sarukkai Chabria is an award-winning poet, writer, translator and anthologist acclaimed for her radical literary aesthetics. Awarded for her Outstanding Contribution to Literature, she presents her widely anthologized work worldwide. She edits *Poetry at Sangam*.

Bernice Chauly is a Malaysian poet, novelist, educator and curator, and the author of seven books of poetry and prose.

David Clarke's first pamphlet, *Gaud*, won the Michael Marks award in 2013. His subsequent collections, *Arc* and *The Europeans*, were both published by Nine Arches Press. A further pamphlet, *Scare Stories*, appeared with V Press.

Aidan Coleman is an early career researcher at the JM Coetzee Centre for Creative Practice at the University of Adelaide. His third book of poems, *Mount Sumptuous* (2020), is published by Wakefield Press.

Katharine Coles' seventh collection of poetry *Wayward* was published in 2019; her memoir *Look Both Ways* in 2018. She is Distinguished Professor at the University of Utah.

Paul Collis is a Barkindji person from the Darling River in north-west New South Wales. His novel *Dancing Home* (UQP) won the David Unaipon Award in 2017.

Oliver Comins lives in West London. Templar Poetry published his collection *Oak Fish Island* in 2018. A Mandeville Press pamphlet, *Playing out time in an awkward light*, appeared in 1992.

Tricia Dearborn is an award-winning Sydney poet, writer and editor. Her latest collections are the critically acclaimed *Autobiochemistry* and the chapbook *She Reconsiders Life on the Run*, both published in 2019. Find her on Twitter @TriciaDearborn and Facebook.

Tjawangwa Dema is the author of two books of poetry, most recently *The Careless Seamstress* which won the Sillerman First Book Prize. She is an Honorary Senior Research Associate at the University of Bristol.

Maura Dooley's most recent collections are *The Silvering* (Bloodaxe) and *Negative of a Group Photograph* (Bloodaxe) (with Elhum Shakerifa) of work by the exiled Iranian poet Azita Ghahreman. She teaches at Goldsmiths, University of London and is a Fellow of the Royal Society of Literature.

Tishani Doshi is an Indian poet, journalist and dancer based in Chennai. Her first poetry collection, Countries of the Body, won the 2006 Forward Poetry Prize for best first collection.

Ian Duhig has won the Forward Best Poem Prize once and the National Poetry Competition twice. He is currently preparing his Selected Poems.

Rachel Blau DuPlessis is the author of the long poem *Drafts*, the collage poem *NUMBERS*, and critical considerations of poetry and gender.

Anne Elvey is author of *On arrivals of breath* (2019), *White on White* (2018) and *Kin* (2014). She holds honorary appointments at Monash University and University of Divinity.

Marjorie Evasco's books have won the National Book Awards for poetry, oral history, biography, and art. She is a University Fellow and Professor Emeritus (Literature) of De La Salle University.

D.W. Fenza is the author of *The Interlude*, a book-length poem. He is the former executive director of the Association of Writers & Writing Programs (AWP), an American organization of creative writing programs and teachers of creative writing.

Martin Figura was some years ago described in a hospital referral letter as 'a pleasant 58 year old gentleman'. He lives in Norwich with Helen Ivory and sciatica. www.martinfigura.co.uk

Caren Florance is a typo-bibliographic artist, exploring the overlaps of visual poetry and text art. Her vispo book, *Lost in Case*, was published by Cordite Books in 2019. Her work is in national and international gallery, library and private collections. www.carenflorance.com

Es Foong is a flash fashionista and spoken word performer living in Naarm (Melbourne). Her poems appear in *Australian Poetry Journal* and *Cold Mountain Review*. She is online at waffleirongirl.com.

Cliff Forshaw's collections include *Vandemonian* (Arc, 2013), *Pilgrim Tongues* (Wrecking Ball, 2015) and *Satyr* (Shoestring, 2017). Cliff is a Royal Literary Fund fellow at York University and also a painter.

Anne-Marie Fyfe (*b.* Cushendall, Co. Antrim) lives in London, runs readings and classes, and has published five poetry collections and a memoir, *No Far Shore: Charting Unknown Waters* (Seren, 2019).

Angela Gardner is an award-winning poet. Her work has appeared in *Meanjin, Cordite, Poetry Wales, ARC* and *Yale Review*. Her eighth book is *Some Sketchy Notes on Matter*.

Philip Gross has published some twenty collections of poetry and won major prizes, but sees most hope in his collaborations with writers, scientists, musicians and visual artists of all kinds.

Nathalie Handal is the author of seven poetry collections including *Life in a Country Album*, and eight plays. Her non-fiction has appeared in *Vanity Fair, The Guardian, The New York Times*, among others.

Oz Hardwick's work has been published and performed internationally in and on diverse media. His chapbook *Learning to Have Lost* (IPSI, 2018) won the 2019 Rubery International Book Award for a poetry collection.

Jennifer Harrison is a contemporary Australian poet, psychiatrist and photographer. She is a recipient of the Christopher Brennan Award.

Ramona Herdman's latest pamphlet, *A warm and snouting thing*, was published by The Emma Press in September 2019. Her previous pamphlet, *Bottle* (HappenStance Press), was a PBS Pamphlet Choice.

Paul Hetherington has published numerous books and won or been shortlisted for more than 20 national and international awards and competitions. He is Professor of Writing at the University of Canberra and head of the International Poetry Studies Institute (IPSI) there.

Tammy Lai-Ming Ho is the Founding Co-editor of *Cha* and *Hong Kong Studies*. She is an Associate Professor at Hong Kong Baptist University and the President of PEN Hong Kong.

Ranjit Hoskote is a poet, cultural theorist and curator based in Bombay. His collections of poetry include *Vanishing Acts* (Penguin, 2006), *Central Time* (Penguin/ Viking, 2014), and *Jonahwhale* (Penguin/ Hamish Hamilton, 2018).

Joshua Ip is an award-winning Singaporean poet, editor and literary organiser. He has published four poetry collections, edited nine anthologies, and co-founded Sing Lit Station, an over-active literary charity. www.joshuaip.com

Helen Ivory is a poet and visual artist. Her fifth Bloodaxe Books collection is *The Anatomical Venus*. She edits the webzine *Ink Sweat and Tears* and teaches online for UEA/NCW.

Andy Jackson's most recent collection, *Music our bodies can't hold*, consists of portrait poems of other people with Marfan Syndrome, and was shortlisted for the John Bray Poetry Award.

Gopika Jadeja is a bi-lingual poet and translator from India, writing in English and Gujarati. She is currently working on a project of English translations of poetry from Gujarat.

Jill Jones' books include *A History of What I'll Become*, and *Viva the Real*, shortlisted for the 2019 Prime Minister's Literary Awards and the 2020 John Bray Poetry Award. *The Beautiful Anxiety* won the 2015 Victorian Premier's Prize for Poetry.

Ilya Kaminsky is a USSR-born, Ukrainian-Russian-Jewish-American poet, critic, translator and professor. He is best-known for his poetry collections *Dancing in Odessa* and *Deaf Republic*, which have earned him several awards.

Mookie Katigbak-Lacuesta is the author of three poetry collections: *The Proxy Eros, Burning Houses* and *Hush Harbor*. In 2015, she completed a writing residency for the International Writing Program at the University of Iowa.

Born in Wales, **Stephen Knight** is the author of a novel and several collections of poems, the latest of which, *Drizzle Mizzle Downpour Deluge*, is published by CB Editions (2020).

Desmond Kon has authored seventeen books, spanning fiction, non-fiction, and poetry. A former journalist, he has edited over twenty books. Founding editor of Squircle Line Press, he can be found at: desmondkon.com

Lydia Kwa has published four novels and two books of poetry. She lives and works on the unceded and traditional territories of the Coast Salish peoples.

Theophilus Kwek has published five volumes of poetry and was shortlisted twice for the Singapore Literature Prize. His next collection, *Moving House*, is forthcoming from Carcanet Press, UK.

Penelope Layland is a Canberra poet and former journalist and speechwriter. Her most recent book is *Things I've Thought to Tell You Since I Saw You Last* (Recent Work Press).

Michael Leach is a Bendigo-based poet and researcher. His poems reside in such journals as *Cordite, Meniscus,* and *MJA*. Michael's debut poetry collection – a chapbook – is forthcoming from Melbourne Poets Union.

Katherine Lockton is a Latinx poet and editor. She has been featured in publications such as *The Spectator* and *The Dark Horse*. She teaches creative writing to children, teenagers and adults.

Glyn Maxwell is a British poet, playwright, novelist, librettist, and lecturer. His next book of poetry, *How The Hell Are You*, will be published by Picador in 2020.

Ian McMillan is a poet and broadcaster from South Yorkshire. He's presented BBC Radio 3's *The Verb* since 2002, and he's currently writing new poems and working with composers on the word/music interface.

Christopher Merrill is the author of many books of poetry and prose, including *Boat* and *The Tree of the Doves: Ceremony, Expedition, War*. He directs Iowa's International Writing Program.

Alyson Miller teaches writing and literature at Deakin University, Melbourne. Her publications include three books of prose poetry, *Dream Animals*, *Pika-Don* and *Strange Creatures*, as well as a critical monograph, *Haunted by Words: Scandalous Texts*.

Jazz Money is an award-winning poet, filmmaker and educator of Wiradjuri and European heritage, currently living on the sovereign lands of the Gundungurra and Darug nations.

Helen Mort lives in Sheffield, England. She has published two collections with Chatto & Windus, *Division Street* and *No Map Could Show Them*. Her work has been shortlisted for the Costa Prize and the T.S. Eliot Prize.

Graham Mort lives in North Yorkshire and is Professor of Creative Writing and Transcultural Literature at Lancaster University. His latest poetry book is *Black Shiver Moss* (Seren 2017).

Paul Munden is a poet and screenwriter based in North Yorkshire. Formerly the Director of The National Association of Writers in Education (NAWE), he is an Adjunct Associate Professor at the University of Canberra.

Marc Nair is a poet who works at the intersection of various art forms. He is currently pursuing projects that involve photography, movement and creative non-fiction. He has published ten collections of poetry.

Pooja Nansi is a poet and performer. Her key works include *Love Is An Empty Barstool* and *Thick Beats for Good Girls*. She is the current festival director of the Singapore Writers Festival.

Katrina Naomi's poetry has appeared on Poems on the Underground (London), in *The TLS* and *The Poetry Review*, and on BBC Radio 4. Her third collection, *Wild Persistence*, will be published by Seren in June 2020. She lives in Cornwall.

K A Nelson won the Overland's Judith Wright Poetry Prize in 2010. Recent Work Press published her first collection, *Inlandia*, in 2018. She was Guest Editor for *Not Very Quiet* online journal for women's poetry in 2019.

Gemma Nethercote Way lives in Canberra. Her poetry has been published in *Meniscus* and *Not Very Quiet*.

Nessa O'Mahony is from Dublin. She has published five books of poetry, the latest being *The Hollow Woman on the Island* (Salmon Poetry, 2019). She co-edited, with Paul Munden, *Metamorphic: 21st century poets respond to Ovid* (Recent Work Press, 2017).

Nathanael O'Reilly's books include *(Un)belonging, Preparations for Departure, Distance, Cult, Suburban Exile* and *Symptoms of Homesickness*. His poetry has appeared in journals and anthologies published in twelve countries.

Moya Pacey's latest collection is *Black Tulips* (Recent Work Press, 2017). She is a founding editor of the online journal notveryquiet.com.

Alvin Pang has been published internationally in more than twenty languages. A poet and editor based in Singapore, he appears in the *Oxford Companion to Modern Poetry in English* and the *Penguin Book of the Prose Poem*. His latest titles include *What Happened: Poems 1997-2017* (Math Paper Press, 2017) and *Uninterrupted Time* (Recent Work Press, 2019).

Robert Pinsky is an American poet, essayist, literary critic, and translator. His most recent book of poems is *At The Foundling Hospital*.

Hamid Roslan's work may be found in *The Volta, Asymptote*, and the *Quarterly Literary Review Singapore*, among others. *parsetreeforestfire* (Ethos Books, 2019) is his debut poetry collection.

Miles Salter has published two collections of poetry, fronts the band Miles and The Chain Gang, and presents The Arts Show on Jorvik Radio. He lives in York, North Yorkshire.

Shane Strange's first collection of poetry *All Suspicions Have Been Confirmed* will be released in late 2020. He is publisher at Recent Work Press and has been Festival Director of the *Poetry on the Move* poetry festival since 2018.

Matthew Stewart works in the Spanish wine trade and lives between Extremadura and West Sussex. His first full collection is *The Knives of Villalejo* (Eyewear Publishing, 2017).

Cole Swensen is a poet and translator; her work has been awarded the Iowa Poetry Prize, the National Poetry Series, and others. She lives in Paris and Providence, RI, USA.

Robin Thomas has had poems published in a number of magazines. His pamphlet *A Fury of Yellow* (Eyewear*)* and his collection *Momentary Turmoil* (Cinnamon) were published in 2016 and 2018.

Hsien Min Toh has published four books of poetry, most recently *Dans quel sens tombent les feuilles* (Paris, 2016).

Jen Webb is Dean of Graduate Research at the University of Canberra, where she writes poetry and researches creativity and culture. Her most recent poetry collections are *Sentences from the Archive*, and *Moving Targets* (Recent Work Press, 2016, 2018).

Susan Wicks's eighth collection is *Dear Crane* (Bloodaxe, 2020). Her first collection, *Singing Underwater* (Faber), won the Aldeburgh Poetry Festival Prize. Her work [as poet and translator] has been shortlisted for many major awards.

Jessica L. Wilkinson is the author of three poetic biographies, most recently *Music Made Visible: A Biography of George Balanchine* (Vagabond Press, 2019). She teaches Creative Writing at RMIT University.

Jordan Williams is a Canberra creative artist who works in text and its materiality, and in combination with digital media and textiles.

Alice Willitts: poet and plantswoman / *Dear,* (Magma, 2019) / MA graduate UEA (2018) / leads the #57 Poetry Collective / co-editor Magma 78: Collaborations / alicewillittspoet.uk

Nicholas Wong is the author of *A Better Way to Say Onlys* (Noemi Press, 2021), and *Crevasse*, the winner of the Lambda Literary Award for Gay Poetry. He is the recipient of the *Australian Book Review*'s Peter Porter Poetry Prize.

John Yau is a poet, fiction writer, art critic, and publisher of Black Square Editions. His books include *Bijoux in the Dark* (2018) and *Genghis Chan on Drums* (forthcoming, 2021). He lives in New York City.

Yeow Kai Chai has two poetry collections, *Pretend I'm Not Here* (2006) and *Secret Manta* (2001). He was Festival Director of Singapore Writers Festival from 2015 to 2018.

Alfred A. Yuson of Manila has authored over 30 books of poetry, fiction, essays, travel, children's literature, and biographies. Among many distinctions, he has received the SEAWrite Award for lifetime achievement.

More Anthologies from Recent Work Press

Giant Steps: Fifty Poets Reflect on the Apollo 11 Moon Landing and Beyond

Metamorphic: 21st Century Poets Respond to Ovid

Abstractions

Poet to Poet: Contemporary Women Poets from Japan

recentworkpress.com

www.ingramcontent.com/pod-product-compliance
Lightning Source LLC
Chambersburg PA
CBHW030256010526
44107CB00053B/1743